Abiding in the Indwelling Trinity

Abiding in the Indwelling Trinity

George A. Maloney

Paulist Press
New York/Mahwah, N.J.

Cover art: Erich Lessing / Art Resource, NY. Greco, El (1541–1614). *The Trinity,* 1577–79. The first work El Greco painted in Toledo for the convent church of Santo Domingo el Antiguo. Museo del Prado, Madrid, Spain.

Scripture extracts are taken from the New Revised Standard Version with Apocrypha, copyright © 1989, by the Division of Christian Education of the National Council of the Churches of Christ in the United States of America and reprinted by permission of the publisher.

Cover design by Sharyn Banks
Book design by Lynn Else

Copyright © 2004 by the Wisconsin Province of the Society of Jesus

IMPRIMI POTEST: Rev. James E. Grummer, SJ
                  Provincial of Wisconsin Jesuit Province
                  The eve of All Saints, October 31, 2001

All rights reserved. No part of this book may be reproduced or transmitted in any form or by any means, electronic or mechanical, including photocopying, recording, or by any information storage and retrieval system without permission in writing from the Publisher.

Library of Congress Cataloging-in-Publication Data

Maloney, George A., 1924–
    Abiding in the indwelling Trinity / George A. Maloney.
        p. cm.
    Includes bibliographical references.
    ISBN 0-8091-4241-4 (alk. paper)
    1. Spirituality—Catholic Church. 2. Trinity. 3. Catholic Church—Doctrines.
I. Title.

BX2350.65.M3325 2004
231'.044—dc22

2004020823

Published by Paulist Press
997 Macarthur Boulevard
Mahwah, New Jersey 07430

www.paulistpress.com

Printed and bound in the
United States of America

Contents

1. Call to Mysticism 1
2. The Community of Divine Love 12
3. The Father Begets His Son 27
4. The Holy Spirit in the Trinity 36
5. The Mystery of the Incarnation 44
6. God's Exploding Love 57
7. I Am the Vine—You Are the Branches 72
8. I Am Crucified with Christ 83
9. The Eucharist and the Holy Trinity 93
10. May Your Joy Be Full 106
11. How to Live in the Indwelling Trinity 118
12. Heaven Bound 153
Notes 176

Dedication

I would like to dedicate this work to my two dear friends, Ray Miles and his wife Andi. Once I was very "computer unfriendly." These very patient friends helped me to a "conversion," so now I am very "computer friendly"! But still I cry out from the depths of my being at times for their very generous help, and they come quickly to my rescue!

Acknowledgments

I am grateful to June Culver for helping to find certain out-of-print works used in this book; to Gladys Stewart for her skillful proofreading and correcting of the manuscript; and to Marge, assistant librarian at the Sisters of St. Joseph of Orange's excellent library, who helped me find many books useful in writing this work.

So then come and place yourself with us

on the mountain of divine knowledge of divine contemplation

and together let us hear the Father's voice—O alas!

How far are we from divine dignity!

How far are we from eternal life!

Even if we should affirm in a contradictory way that we abide in Him

and we possess in us Him who abides in unapproachable light,

who also entirely remains and abides in us,

and yet we would wish, seated in the bowels of the earth,

to philosophize on things that transcend this earth....

But, O my Christ, deliver those who are tied to You from vanity and pride.

Make us participators in your sufferings and your glory

and deign to make us never to be separated from You,

now and in the future world to come,

forever and ever. Amen[1]

                St. Symeon the New Theologian (d. 1022)

CHAPTER ONE

Call to Mysticism

The Grail legend, written centuries ago by Chrétien de Troyes, is about the Holy Grail, the chalice used by Jesus at the Last Supper. It is kept in a castle in the care of a king, called the Fisher King. The king had been severely wounded in his adolescence and lies on a litter. It had been prophesized that he would be healed by the Grail when an innocent fool comes to the castle.

Most of us have followed in storybook form the wanderings and adventures of Parsifal, the hero of the legend. If he asks the right question—"Whom does the Grail serve?"—Parsifal will be able to heal the king. But alas, he forgets the question upon first meeting the king. After more wanderings, Parsifal goes to confession on Good Friday. He is reconciled to God, remembers the right question, and then sets off for the castle. However, this is where the author decided to end the story.

Down through the ages authors have made attempts to finish the tale. One attempt has Parsifal asking the right question: "Whom does the Grail serve?" The answer is given: "The Grail serves the Grail King." He has lived in the central room of the castle from time immemorial. The sick king of the castle is healed at once, and all his people live in peace and joy.[1]

Most of us human beings live our lives in search of the Grail. We see it as a goal that will bring us happiness. When we can forget our own petty interests and pursuits, when we have silenced our own clamorings for instant happiness, we can then ask the right question. We shall learn that the Grail does not exist for us, but solely for the Grail King.

Self-Fulfillment

Like Parsifal, we are lonely pilgrims on a quest. We burn with the thirst to become complete, whole, integrated persons. We travel through life's experiences, looking for happiness. Something in us pushes us onward in our quest, something that's always gnawing at the core of our being, leaving us unfulfilled. We try the pleasures of this world like a child who gleefully stretches out to grasp glittering soap bubbles. But we stand on the brink of despair, clutching a handful of nothingness.

We think honors, wealth, and power can bring an end to that inner malaise. Perhaps knowledge or professional work or involvement in social causes can bring those inner yearnings to satisfying fulfillment. Yet like King Solomon we, too, can readily admit: "Then I considered all that my hands had done and the toil I had spent in doing it, and again, all was vanity and a chasing after wind" (Eccl 2:11).

Made by God for God

For most of us, it takes several years of such futile searching to realize that nothing in the whole world can ever satisfy us but God. For it is God who has given us this basic drive to possess him and to be possessed by him. Never on earth has there been a human being that found full self-actualization in the sole possession of material things or even in the service for individual human beings. This is the way God has created man and woman—to find themselves in relation to other knowing and loving beings. And through such love relationships we are to discover the loving beauty of God himself.

In surrendering to another and ultimately to God in unselfish love, we reach the highest state of communication. Through faith in prayer, we come to know experientially God's personal love for us individually. We can move ourselves toward beauty itself, toward the Absolute, the transcendent God, who comes to us in a tender, but infinite Love. St. Augustine kept searching for the Grail to bring him happiness, while all the time the Grail King lived in the center of his heart. Augustine discovered that the Grail did not exist to bring him happiness, but that it existed, as he himself existed, to serve the King, who lived in the inner mansion of his own heart:

> Too late have I loved Thee, O Thou, Beauty of ancient days, yet ever new! Too late I loved Thee! And behold, Thou were within and I abroad, and there I searched for Thee; deformed, I plunging amid those fair forms which Thou hast made. Thou wert with me, but I was not with Thee, which unless they were in Thee, were not at all.[2]

Thirst for God

God has made us human beings according to his image and likeness (Gen 1:26–27). We are destined to grow in greater knowledge and love of the trinitarian community of love. Their loving presence as personalized relations of uncreated energies of love surrounds us, permeates us, bathes us constantly in their great loving communication of God the Father through his Son in his Spirit.

As we become present in knowledge and love to God-Trinity's loving presence, the seeds that God planted in us gradually grow to fulfillment. We are being driven into the silent desert of our hearts to receive God's Word, who will reveal our true dignity to be with him, children of God (Rom 8:15; Gal 4:6). In such silence and inner poverty, we learn to "hear" God's word from within us.

Emil Brunner describes this call to our true existence: The being of a human being as an "I" is being from and in the Divine Word, whose claim "calls" us human beings into existence.[3]

My Flesh Longs for You

God is always calling us to consent to be swept up into the trinitarian life, and we alone can reply as we cooperate freely with God's gift of sanctifying grace through the Holy Spirit. Our answer fulfills the purpose for which we were made, or we destroy ourselves as human persons. This "existential longing" to be what God wants us to be, in knowing and loving communication with him, is at the heart of our being truly human. It is a yearning to become "whole" and fulfilled. It is a longing that the image of God in us will reach its full fruition.

Many human beings thirst for God only when they have fallen to the depths of human degradation and frustration. Others thirst for God because in the gift of prayer God has revealed himself in a partial vision of his perfect beauty, along with the vivid experience of their own emptiness apart from God: "My soul thirsts for God, for the living God. When shall I come and behold the face of God?" (Ps 42:2).

Prayer: Key to Transcendence

Prayer is the art whereby we human beings communicate with God in knowledge and love. We lift our minds and our hearts toward God. But more, we pray, not primarily to receive gifts from God, but to surrender as a self-giving gift to him, Jesus Christ, who has given us everything. Prayer is our avenue to enter into God's timeless and infinite, personal and perfect love for each of us individually. Prayer raises our consciousness to the primal experience that is the beginning and the end of all reality, namely, being grasped by God, known and loved uniquely by him so that in such a re-creating experience, we rise to new levels of spiritual perfection.

What Is Mysticism?

Starved for an immediate experience in the deepest reaches of their consciousness, many Westerners are turning to the Absolute with a frenetic vengeance that at times reaches pathetic proportions. It is a thirst for religious experiences and the world of the "spirit." M. C. Richards, artisan and poet, in her book *The Crossing Point* expresses this inner hunger:

> One of the truths of our time is [that] this hunger is found deep in people all over the planet for coming into relationships with each other. Human consciousness is crossing a threshold as mighty as the one from the Middle Ages to the Renaissance. People are hungering and thirsting after experience that feels true to them on the inside after so much hard work mapping the outer spaces of the physical world. They are gaining courage to ask for what they need: living interconnections, a sense of individual worth, shared opportunities.[4]

Decline of Inner Experience

In our dehumanized, rationalistic world, we are rich in techniques but poor in intuition, in feminine receptivity to the inner voice that resides within, in the "temple invisible." Yet we see everywhere the reaction to a technical world that places supreme values on the laws of the observable as the only index of reality. We are crying out to understand ourselves as unique persons discovered in the intimacy of an I-Thou loving relationship that will drive away the fearful, solitary loneliness of a person reduced to a digit or a statistic.

Such stress on objective knowledge has lessened or completely obliterated any realization of the mystery of our inner life with its experiences of God's graces and his redemptive, healing love. The most fascinating inner world lies within all of us, where the Divine Trinity dwells in loving oneness with us, and yet most of us are hardly aware of all this inner richness and beauty, beyond an intellectual assent given to a truth revealed by God through his Church. In the words of the poet Gerard Manley Hopkins, SJ, "......these things, these things were always there, but for the beholder."[5]

God Is Love by Nature

St. John writes in his first epistle: "God is love, and those who abide in love abide in God, and God abides in them" (1 John 4:16). If God is love by nature, then he is always seeking by his nature to share his being by communicating his presence. In Christianity, God becomes a God toward us by communicating himself through his Word in his Spirit of Love. God creates the entire world as good, as a sign of his burning desire to give himself in faithful communication through his Word.

The world at its interior and within each of us is filled with the self-communicating Trinity. God is filling the universe and ourselves with his loving Self. God is Love and is "nowhere," since he is everywhere. His uncreated energies of Love swirl through and fill all creatures with his loving, creative presence. God delights to give himself as a triune community to us human beings. "I love those who love me, and those who seek me diligently find me" (Prov 8:17).

Taste and See the Sweetness of the Lord

In all human beings there exists a propensity toward mysticism. We have within ourselves an inner drive toward union with the Supreme Reality. If we call that Reality God, we are saying that all other finite beings must ultimately fail to satisfy our thirst for deeper, more intense interpenetration with God.

All of us have enjoyed moments of ecstatic human love, a gasp of awe at some breathtaking natural beauty, or a lifting of ourselves out of our habitual mode of perceiving the real world around us and an entering into a world of seemingly greater simplification while listening to transcendent music. Still, no matter how common the experience of transcendent oneness is among us, *mysticism* is one of the most misunderstood words in our human vocabulary.

Evelyn Underhill, a renowned English authority on mysticism, describes it:

> Mysticism is the expression of the innate yearning of the human spirit toward total harmony with the transcendental order, whatever may be the theological formula in which this order is expressed. This yearning with the great mystics gradually takes possession of the whole field of consciousness; it domi-

nates their whole life and attains its climax in that experience called mystic union, whether it be with the God of Christianity, the World Soul of pantheism or the Absolute of philosophy.

This desire for union and straining toward it inasmuch as they are vital and real (not purely speculative) constitute the real subject of mysticism. Through this, the human consciousness reaches its further and richest development.[6]

A Christian Mysticism

By our baptism we are all called to enter into a oneness in love with the three Persons of the indwelling Trinity. In authentic Christian mystical experiences there are two important constitutive elements. The first is the transcendent, totally "Other," given by revelation in holy scripture and through Christian tradition, of God as the Source from whom all other forms of existence flow and to whom all beings return in a hunger and thirst toward greater union. God as transcendent is other than we are: incomprehensible, unpossessable, unchanging, eternal in his perfections, completely holy, and independent of all outside forces. He is the fire from which all sparks come, an abyss of infinity separating himself from the created world.

Such a mystical experience is an immediate and experiential perception of God substantially present in the just soul as object of its knowledge and love. The transcendent God is also the immanent God in whom "we live and move and have our being" (Acts 17:28). He is not an object outside of us. He is an encompassing, loving energy that permeates each cell of our being. In St. Augustine's words, "He is more intimate to me than I to myself."[7]

It is Christian mysticism that combines the nonduality immanence of the Far Eastern religions with the transcendence of a God as being external to the subject and revealing himself through the medium of prophets, as found predominantly in such prophetic religions as Judaism and Islam. Such new knowledge and wisdom come to the Christian mystic as a gift of faith, hope, and love infused into the individual by God's Holy Spirit. There is no other way of dealing with his light; the mystic sees as did the prophets of old. When God touches us with his light, we then know that God knows us. He who sees God knows that God sees him. And he knows that he knows God.

An Indwelling Presence

The indwelling presence of the Trinity as light within the justified Christian permeates the whole being; it integrates the body, soul, and spirit levels into a whole human being, consumed by love for God. We see his light everywhere, adore him in great humble thanksgiving, and abandon ourselves totally in complete service to do God's holy will. We are instructed by God-Trinity in the things of God. Above all, we know at each moment what is the will of God for us. Christian mysticism relates the individual to the historical perspective and to the world community into which the individual person strives for fidelity to cooperate in each moment with the divine will, "so that you may discern what is the will of God—what is good and acceptable and perfect" (Rom 12:2).

As Christians of deeper prayer are led progressively into the inner meaning of reality, they are not led away from the created world. Rather, they are led into reverence and worship of God as present everywhere *within* the created world.

The flowers, trees, birds, animals, the beauties of each new season, the sun, moon, stars, the mountains, lakes, oceans: the entire world reveals to them the loving, active presence of God-Trinity. They are thus concerned to give the Heavenly Father, through the Son, by the sanctifying bond of Divine Love, the Holy Spirit in all of God's creatures, all glory and praise as they seek to return love for love.

Direct and Immediate Experiences

The true test of how we live in this I-Thou-We-Community of love activity within us is measured by the great joy we manifest to God and neighbor as we seek to radiate our absolute surrender in loving God and all other human persons we are privileged to serve. Our union with God-Trinity will make our joys more pure and unto God's eternal glory.

Christian mystics seem to have been given new eyes and ears, interior senses that allow them to meet God in a direct, immediate way of perceiving. Walter Hilton, the fourteenth-century English mystic, writes:

> This tasting of manna is an awareness of the life of grace, which comes from the opening of the soul's eyes. And this grace does not differ from the grace that the elect soul feels at the beginning of one's conversion. It is the same grace, but experienced in another way.[8]

Knowledge Without an Intermediary

The authentic mystic has knowledge of God without any intermediary, while the nonmystic approaches God as an object to discuss. There may be some feeling of God, but not a "touching" and a "tasting" him as real, close, intimately dwelling within. Nonmystics can talk about God and encounter him in prayer through ideas, images, and concepts. They are able to know God, but in and through something that is not God himself. There is always a great distance separating God from them. This is usually also the manner in which they experience other human persons, in an objective, judgmental way. As one prays, so one lives; as one lives, so one prays.

For true mystics, the veil is lifted. The wall of ideas and affections falls and the mystics "see" and "feel" God with an intimate and direct certainty. Dag Hammarskjold (d. 1961), former Secretary General of the UN, attests to the truth of this statement as he wrote in his diary, *Markings:*

> Then I saw that the wall had never been there, that the "unheard-of" is here and this, not something and somewhere else, that the "offering is" and now, always and everywhere—"surrendered" to be what, in me, God gives of himself to himself.[9]

Chapter Two

The Community of Divine Love

If we are to be made "participants of the divine nature" (2 Pet 1:4), it must come about by the strong, persistent love of God, who cloaks himself in deep silence before our selfish, bombastic questionings about God, ourselves, and our world. We have been made by God for communion, a "union with" God and all human beings.

Another way of putting it is to describe God as a loving community of persons who wish to share their trinitarian life as we experience their Divine Love in each event of each day. We begin to move toward loving communion with God and neighbor by means of "communication." The first step of communication is to relay information to another on a linear level. Such knowledge tends to deal with logical facts, ideas that are comprehensible to our human reasoning. Our sciences are examples of such communication. Making theology exclusively a "science" is another example of such knowledge.

Language of the Heart

But there is a higher level of knowledge that is communicable. This is communion between friends and lovers, between ourselves and our loving God. It is the language of the human heart in which love mysteriously speaks and makes the loved one present as a gift to the other.

There can be no array of logical proof that will ever bring about such a communion. It is a surrendering love built upon faith and hope in the one loved. We can say that we human beings have been made by God to become "present" to the trinitarian community of love that is "poured into our hearts through the Holy Spirit that has been given to us," as Paul writes in Romans 5:5.

We have been made by God for love, for communion with God and the whole world in the unity of God's Word. This is the great craving placed into our hearts by God. This, we could say, is the presence of God as uncreated energies of love, moving us by his Spirit toward greater and greater union with God and all of God's creation.

Living in the third millennium, we stand before God and shout out with rage our demands that he speak to us as we would wish him to speak. But all we hear in reply is the echo of our own anger. We have effectively lost the ability to recognize the voice of God as he speaks his Word to us in silence and in love. We hear instead the insidious promptings of the demonic within us that, like a boa constrictor, wraps itself around our throats and suffocates us in a kind of living death. Such is the only silence most of us ever experience. It is the silence created by the absence of speech and the lack of true communication in love between us and God and all other human persons.

Create Silence

Søren Kierkegaard, the great Danish philosopher, wrote about genuine silence and the urgency on our part to attain it:

> The present state of the world and the whole of life are diseased. If I were a doctor and were asked for my advice, I should reply: Create Silence! Bring

human beings to silence. The Word of God cannot be heard in the noisy world of today. And even if it were blazoned forth with all the panoply of noise so that it could be heard in the midst of all the other noise, then it would no longer be the Word of God. Therefore, create silence.[1]

In loving another, we become a gifted presence to that person. We wish to live in union, the true meaning of communion, with that person so as to be present as often and as intimate as possible, not only physically in space and time, but also more importantly in the inner recesses of our consciousness. We are participants of the divine nature (2 Pet 1:4) because God is love (1 John 4:8).

The Trinitarian Community of Love

God the Father, in absolute silence, in a communication of love impossible for us human beings to understand, speaks his one eternal Word through his Spirit of Love. In that one Word, the Father is perfectly present, totally self-giving to his Son. "For in him the whole fullness of deity dwells bodily" (Col 2:9). But in his Spirit, the Father also hears his Word come back to him in a perfect, eternal "yes" of total, surrendering love that is again the Holy Spirit.

The Trinity is a reciprocal community of a movement of the Spirit of Love between Father and Son. Our weak minds cannot fathom the peace and joy, the ardent excitement and exuberant self-surrender that flow in a reposeful motion between Father and Son through the silent Holy Spirit. God becomes real only because he can communicate in love through his Word. His Word gives him his identity as Father. But that means eternal self-giving to the Other, his Word in Love, the Holy Spirit.

An Apophatic Approach Is Needed

Whatever human words may be used to penetrate somewhat the inner mystery of God's nature as love in a communion of persons, our attitude demands something of the "apophatic" approach as described in Chapter 1. This is more than a negation of whatever we can positively assert through rational knowledge about the attributes of God. Apophatic knowledge is knowledge given to us by the Holy Spirit that goes beyond all human knowledge (Eph 3:17–18).

The Eastern Greek Fathers learned well from holy scripture and from their own sense of brokenness in prayer that only God can lead us into the mystery of God's nature as love. We must realize that we cannot comprehend God's inner life completely, or we would have to be part of the family of God by our very nature.

Scripture insists that we can know this Trinity by a "not knowing." In our poverty and utter creatureliness, in our sinfulness and alienation from the heavenly Father, we realize that to know God is beyond our power. "No one has ever seen God. It is God the only Son, who is close to the Father's heart, who has made him known" (John 1:18).

Yet the Good News revealed by the Word made flesh, Jesus Christ, is that we can come to know the Father through the Son: "And this is eternal life, that they may know you, the only true God, and Jesus Christ whom you have sent" (John 17:3). As we Christians grow in contemplation, we realize more and more that God must reveal himself to us. We can only wait in the desert of our nothingness, hoping to receive God as he wishes to make himself known to us.

With the humility of children, we seek entrance into the heart of God as he communicates himself to his Word through his Spirit of Love. This is the teaching of Jesus who speaks about the possibility of such children receiving, not merely knowledge or a communication, but the privilege in contemplation to enter into the very trinitarian "communion": "I thank you, Father, Lord of heaven and earth, because you have hidden these things from the wise and the intelligent and have revealed them to infants" (Matt 11:25).

Experiencing the Indwelling Trinity

God's Word incarnate, Jesus Christ, by his death and resurrection is now a living Word dwelling within us along with his Holy Spirit. He not only gives us the elements that constitute God's inner life, but he also makes it possible through his Spirit that those elements can be experienced by us.

The doctrine of the Trinity is not only what makes Christianity uniquely different from all other religions, but it is a reality that effects the fulfillment of our very being as human persons. Christology and all other dogmas, liturgy and the sacraments, preaching the Gospel and developing the Christian life of Christlike virtues—all have their meaning in and are subordinated to this central teaching of the Trinity.

We are baptized in the love and power of the Father, Son, and Spirit. We profess in faith that, even as infants, we were receiving God's trinitarian actions upon us. We have been confirmed, reconciled to God. Some were ordained, others married. All have been forgiven sins and healed in the name of the three divine Persons. We bless ourselves in the Trinity. and we seek to do all for the glory of the Trinity.

God revealed this mystery to us in order that he might share the secret of his own intimate life with us. This reality is meant in God's salvific plan to be a living experience. We are to live in this teaching's reality. But unfortunately, for too many centuries, the precision of professional theologians has dominated our approach to the Trinity. We were rooted more in Aristotelian philosophy than in holy scripture. It is God's living Word who alone can reveal to us this awesome reality and make it effective and transformative in our lives.

The Richness of the Godhead

In God we see that silence is not opposed to words, but true Word-communication comes from the silence of the Spirit of Love, and continues to be spoken and lived out in the same silence of the Spirit. Perhaps a good way to understand God's communicative silence is to study the classic Byzantine icon of the Trinity painted by the Russian monk Andrei Rublev (d. 1430).

This painting is a mystical, apophatic vision, through harmony and relationship of colors and circular lines, of the inner trinitarian life of movement and rest, peace and joy, a community of three-in-one. The Godhead is a nameless form that constantly feeds back through its circular movement from one person to the other two.

At the Oak of Mambre

In Rublev's icon we see three angels, the heavenly visitors to Abraham at the oak of Mambre (Gen 18), depicting the three Persons of the Trinity. The Father is shown as the angel on the left, as a figure subdued and retiring, suggesting the apophatic belief in the direct unknowability of the Father or the Godhead of the Trinity, except through the Son, who is the angelic figure in the center.

The Son dominates the entire icon as he gazes lovingly at the Father, while pointing his two fingers, symbolic of his two natures, divine and human, toward the eucharistic chalice on the white table before them.

The Holy Spirit is seen as the third angel, on the right, dressed in a green cloak, the sign of youth and fullness of powers. Before there are divine Persons, in intercommunion with each other in expressed love, there is the Godhead. The Eastern Fathers begin with the Godhead as the "unoriginated Source," the principal root of unity in the Trinity. St. Gregory of Nazianzus, the great fourth-century Greek theologian who wrote so eloquently about the Trinity, describes the Father as the source and goal of diversity or personal relationships within the Trinity:

> The nature is one in three; it is God; but that which makes the unity is the Father, from whom and to whom the order of persons runs its course, not in such a way that the nature is confused, but that it is possessed without distinction of time or of will or of power.[2]

The Godhead Is "Unnatured Nature"

This Godhead is the Abyss of Silence. It is not a nonbeing out of which comes the being of the three Persons. It is God as "unnatured nature," to use Meister Eckhart's phrase. It is nonbeing, for it contains all beings. It is nowhere, for it cannot be contained in its wildness before it becomes tamed by love. It is the ocean before fish have been created. It is the air before birds have been made to fly. It is the fullness of the Uncreated before the spark ignites and hurls intelligence toward loving union. It is where total poverty meets infinite richness. It is Infinite Zero from which everyone and everything radiates and to which all lovingly return.

Because of the Godhead's infinite richness, it cannot be classified in quantified numbers or in categories of beings that have an origin of their being. The Godhead is beyond all being and yet is found in all being, including the Trinity and ourselves. Nietzsche once wrote: "One must possess a chaos within to give birth to a star."[3] It is here that the Father becomes Father of his Son through the silent love of the Holy Spirit, who proceeds from both the Father and the Son. Two looks devoured by love! It is here that we are led in silent adoration and contemplation to a knowing beyond our knowing.

God Is Not an Object

In silence we come into the Void and merge with the darkness of the Godhead. No longer is God an "object" toward which we go in prayer to communicate in order to receive some "things." The ocean covers everything and does not need to become wet, since all things are wet because of its complete covering of everything.

Like the crackling sound of a fiery spark that shoots through the rain-soaked heavens, a movement stirs within non-movement. A light moves through darkness. Out of the Void God stirs as personal Source, the Father, who wishes from all eternity to share his fullness of being. The Mind wishes to think a thought, to speak a word, in order to know himself as the Begetter of the Word.

The Father moves the Godhead from pure repose and absolute silence to meaningful, loving motion, as he pours the fullness of his divinity into his Son (Col 2:9). What we could never know, God's Word has revealed to us. God is a loving community, a family of loving Persons, each Person receiving his uniqueness by self-emptying gift of total self to the other, in and through the gift of Love itself, the Spirit.

It is an ecstatic, loving intimacy of the Father emptying himself into his Son through his Spirit of Love. Such intimacy and self-emptying are returned by the Son's gifting himself back to the Father through the same Spirit. Jesus reveals that in the Trinity is the secret of life, which unfolds in silence, the language of love. Love is a call to receive one's being in the intimate self-surrendering of the other. In the ecstasy of "standing outside" of oneself and becoming available through the gift of love to live for the other, Father and Son and Holy Spirit, all come into their unique personhood as distinct yet united Persons.[4]

The *I* Is the Child of the *We*

The French philosopher and playwright Gabriel Marcel describes the mystery of true love in the Trinity and in our own human love relations: "The I is the child of the We."[5] God as Trinity is the revelation that uniqueness of persons comes only from a family of two or more persons in love. In the very self-giving of the Father to the Son, and the Son to the Father, a third Person has unique "personhood," the Holy Spirit. He proceeds, not as another Word, but from the silent love of the Father for the Son and the single, silent Word, the Son, surrendering to the Father. The Spirit is silent love, experienced, but not heard except in the soundless of the gift of love itself.

Silence within the Trinity

The awesome mystery of the Trinity, which is the beginning and the end of all reality, reveals to us a transcendent truth that should permeate our entire lives. Out of Absolute Silence the Godhead could not yet experience community. For an I-Thou relationship bringing forth a We-Community could come only when the Father spoke in relative silence his

Word. That "relative" silence we call the Holy Spirit, the binding, self-sacrificing love between the Father and the Son.

The Book of Genesis describes the Holy Spirit as the "cosmic bird" that hovers over the chaos and the void. It stirs the "I" of the heavenly Father to perceive himself, as one not isolated. The Spirit, who is the Spirit of Love, moves the heart of the Father, and the Son is begotten in the silent Word that the Father utters. The Father thrills to see himself imaged, as Mind discovers itself in the Word that issues from the Mind. But he thrills also to discover himself as the unique Father of his Son, when the Son in the power of the silent Spirit utters his silent "yes" in total self-surrender to the Father.

We Are Made in the Image and Likeness of God

In Genesis 1:26–27, we read: "Let us make humankind in our image, according to our likeness...So God created humankind in his image, in the image of God he created them; male and female he created them."

We project that image of God most often, not in the negative silence of chosen isolation and mutism, but in speech. But the words we speak must proceed from the same silent Spirit of Love and return "home" to that Spirit. We move away from imaging God as he speaks his Word in the silent love of the Spirit when we fail to speak out words in God's love.

It is through God's Spirit of Love that he has the name of "Father." His fatherhood is expressed in his silent, eternal, self-giving to his Son. St. Hilary of Poitiers (d. 368) insists that the Father and the Son have a perfect mutual relation of Father and Son to each other.[6] If the Father and Son mutually know themselves, this is brought about necessarily by the Holy Spirit, who allows them in silence, not only to affirm themselves as Father and Son, but also mutually to recognize themselves as such.

An Implosion of Love

From this threefold movement, therefore, all reality within the Trinity and all reality outside in all of creation flows through the Trinity's uncreated energies of love. Such an "implosion" of love between Father and Son through the Spirit within the Trinity seemingly is not enough. Such tremendous love within the Trinity, we learn only from scripture, seeks to "explode" outside of its own community. God freely wishes to create new life that can share in the divine, ecstatic love within the Trinity.

We human beings know this to be our own experience of an authentic I-Thou love relationship; it stretches outward to share that love in new human love with another in the creation of new life. This is true because it is first true of God, the Source of all participated life and love. When we love one another, God's love in us is being perfected (1 John 4:12).

It is only faith received through God's revelation found in the Old and New Testaments that opens us to accept the good news that the trinitarian community of Father, Son, and Holy Spirit moves outward freely to create a world of participated beauty. Yet of all God's material creatures, we human beings are gifted to be able to communicate with the Trinity by sharing in God's very own nature (2 Pet 1:4). We are called in God's gratuitous love to receive the divine, self-emptying love as self-gift of Father and Son and Holy Spirit.

The Divine Economy

We see, therefore, that the ineffable mystery of the Trinity, which escapes our own human comprehension, can, however, be known and experienced in and through Jesus Christ and the Holy Spirit. God not only deemed to reveal the truth of this mystery to us, but also in that revelation he has made the mystery of the Trinity the beginning and end of all reality. God effects our fulfillment precisely in and through the activities of the triune God in the context of our history of salvation.

We come not only to know but also to experience the triune God within what Karl Rahner calls the biblical data about the "economic" Trinity. *"Economia"* (*oikonomia* in Greek) etymologically refers to the well-running of a household.[7] In theology it usually refers to any divine activity in relationship to creatures. Thus theologians speak of "the economy of salvation." Among the Eastern Greek Fathers, "theology" properly concerns itself with teaching about the Divine Being itself, namely the Holy Trinity known in its relation to created beings. This belongs vitally to the realm of the economy of salvation.[8]

Rahner states very emphatically his principle that he maintains is the persistent teaching of the Eastern Greek Fathers of the relationship of the Trinity toward us human beings made in God's image in the history of salvation. He writes: "The 'economic Trinity' is the 'immanent Trinity' and the 'immanent Trinity' is the 'economic Trinity.'"[9] This means that the very relationships within the Trinity (immanent Trinity) are the same relationships of the Trinity in bringing about God's eternal plan of salvation. In identifying the Trinity of the economy of salvation with the very life within the Trinity of Father, Son, and Holy Spirit, Rahner and many contemporary theologians seek to recapture the fundamental teaching of the Eastern Fathers that the personalism of the three Divine Persons toward each other in their self-giving is similar to their self-giving relationships to us human beings.

God Is the Giver and the Gift

If this were not so, God would be the "giver" and not the gift itself. He would give himself only to the extent that he communicates a gift distinct from himself.[10] Upon this Eastern Christian teaching of the similarity between the immanent, "trinitarian activities" and the "economic activities" hinges the answer to the question: Are we human beings so loved by God that we are able to be radically transformed by God's very gift of himself through the Trinity's very own transforming Persons of Father, Son, and Spirit? If God merely loves us to the degree that he gives us created gifts, we would never be truly saved from our sins and be regenerated into true children of God.

Crucial in this patristic doctrine is that, through God's uncreated energies of love,[11] we actually do make contact with the living Trinity, that God truly is love. The community of the Trinity wants to share its perfect love of self-giving within the Trinity with us human beings by transforming us into sharers of God's very own divine nature. St. Irenaeus of the second century describes God as coming toward us in the created world through his two hands, Jesus Christ and the Holy Spirit: "And therefore throughout all time, human beings, having been molded at the beginning by the hands of God, that is, of the Son and the Spirit, are made after the image and likeness of God."[12]

We Are Called by God to Share Divine Life

God is grace! He gives us this sharing in the Trinity's life through the uncreated energies that are the personalized, self-giving of the Father and Son and Holy Spirit to us. It is this moving of God's We-Community toward us that gives us a share in the very life of the three Persons that is at the heart of the Christian message, and that is the chief purpose of Christ's Incarnation, teaching, and death on the cross, and the outpouring of the Holy Spirit.

It is for this reason that the Eastern Christian theologians, mystics that they were, always began with the first words of the Book of Genesis: "In the beginning, God...." It is for this reason that we should be grounded firmly in the great mystery of the Holy Trinity since all other relationships flow out of this mystery. In prayerful humility and a sense of our deep unworthiness to approach God in order to probe into how God communicates himself to us, we turn to that intimate, trinitarian union of love to which God calls us.

It is a path that leads us beyond idols and images, even beyond our objectivizing God as a Person whom we can address as another created being. It is a knowledge of experience that admits of infinite growth because this knowledge surpasses all human understanding and becomes identified with true love. To know the Trinity in this sense of mystery is to love God through the Spirit of Jesus Christ as God loves us.

St. Paul's statement in his Letter to the Ephesians can serve to summarize in nonspeculative, scriptural terms the movement of the divine We-Community into our world in order to share with us human beings the same relationships enjoyed between Father and Son as I-Thou, brought together in perfect, loving union by the Spirit:

ABIDING IN THE INDWELLING TRINITY

Blessed be the God and Father of our Lord Jesus Christ, who has blessed us in Christ with every spiritual blessing in the heavenly places, just as he chose us in Christ before the foundation of the world to be holy and blameless before him in love. He destined us for adoption as his children through Jesus Christ, according to the good pleasure of his will, to the praise of his glorious grace that he freely bestowed on us in the Beloved. In him we have redemption through his blood, the forgiveness of our trespasses, according to the riches of his grace that he lavished on us. With all wisdom and insight he has made known to us the mystery of his will, according to his good pleasure that he set forth in Christ, as a plan for the fullness of time, to gather up all things in him, things in heaven and things on earth. In Christ we have also obtained an inheritance, having been destined according to the purpose of him who accomplishes all things according to his counsel and will, so that we, who were the first to set our hope on Christ, might live for the praise of his glory. In him you also, when you had heard the word of truth, the gospel of your salvation, and had believed in him, were marked with the seal of the promised Holy Spirit; this is the pledge of our inheritance toward redemption as God's own people, to the praise of his glory. (Eph 1:3–14).

CHAPTER THREE

The Father Begets His Son

We receive our existence in and through a human community, the family. It is in a loving community that we best evolve the potential within us to become fully human by discovering our unique identity in a loving I-Thou relationship. The kind of isolation that breeds loneliness not only destroys such a loving community, but also brings destruction to our own entire being as well.

The Inner Desire in Us for Love

We will do just about anything to make contact with another living being, especially another living human being, in order to establish a sharing community. This burning need to communicate with others is the way God made us, so that through communication with others, we might reach some level of communion in love. We have been made by God out of his infinite love to give love and to receive it in return. When this is not actualized, we become dehumanized.

When we were first born, we lived a very primitive sort of existence, following instincts that were basically "self-serving." As we developed—through discipline, education, and social experiences—we discovered ourselves to be subjects, individuals, persons called to make choices in love or out of self-centeredness. We discovered the world of objects "over there," while we were "over here." We maintained certain distinctions between ourselves and "them" by our ability to put other persons and things into rational and impersonal "boxes."

But to all of us there comes the call of God's Spirit of love, inviting us to enter into a higher level of existence where we can experience a higher degree of human consciousness and come to recognize the uniqueness of our own and others' being. At the heart of God is the loving community of the Trinity, for God is love (1 John 4:8).

Love is a call to enter fully into oneself through an intimate surrendering of that self to another. In the ecstasy of "standing outside" of themselves, the three members of the Trinity become available through the gift of love to live for each other in the Trinity—Father, Son, and Holy Spirit. In this way they come to discover themselves as unique, distinct Persons, who are united in passionate self-emptying love. In joyful surrender to one another, the Father and the Son discover their uniqueness in their oneness through the hidden, emptying Spirit of love.

Do We Believe in the True Trinity?

In Karl Rahner's opinion, the majority of Christians objectify the three different Persons in the Divine Trinity.[1] As a result, many Christians do not relate to the Persons of the Trinity as we find revealed in holy scripture and as taught by Jesus himself. Such Christians are quite satisfied with an exclusive concentration on the historical person of Jesus.

The Jesuit theologian Luis M. Bermejo describes such Christians:

> For all practical purposes we seem to have forgotten that Jesus is essentially the mediator to the Father and the immediate source of the bountiful outpouring of

the Holy Spirit....Every spiritual dimension, every angle of our relationship with God is almost mechanically attributed to Jesus. For them Jesus suffices.[2]

St. Paul never stopped with Christ. For Paul, Christ is a mediator who points higher up, to the Father, and who also with the Father dispenses the Spirit to Christ's followers.

Basic Traits of a True, Loving Community

Inspired by the writings of Gabriel Marcel, I have summarized the characteristics of the interpersonalized Trinity of the Father, Son, and Holy Spirit. These are the elements basic to all Divine and human intimate love:

1. Availability
2. Mutuality
3. Sacrifice of oneself as a gift for the happiness of the other

In the Trinity, Jesus reveals to us the secret of all reality and life itself. Love is a call to receive one's unique I-ness in the intimate self-emptying for the other. It is only in interpersonal relationships based on self-sacrificing love as a free gift of oneself to the other and a return to the first giver that God—Father, Son, Holy Spirit—and all created intellectual beings can find each one's own unique personhood. Only such a person is free enough to love others with such "agapic," self-emptying love as the Father and the Son have in their mutual Spirit of love for each other.

Richard of St. Victor (d. 1173)

Perhaps a model proposed by Richard of St. Victor, who was highly influenced by the trinitarian, personal relations as found in the Eastern Greek Fathers, may help us to avoid the scholastic language of viewing the three trinitarian relations and help to approach this mystery with a more biblical and patristic approach.

Richard bases his understanding of the Trinity on the premise that true love seeks to be totally self-sacrificing on behalf of the one loved. But such a love wants to be shared with another, thus an *I* and a *Thou* move into a *We*-Community of three persons equally loving each other with the very same nature of the same, perfect love. He writes:

> When one gives love to another and when he alone loves the other alone, there is love certainly, but not shared love....Strictly speaking, there is shared love when two persons love a third in a harmony of affection and a community of love and when the loves of the two converge in the single flame of love they have for the third....From this, then, it is evident that shared love would not have a place in the divinity if there were only two persons and not a third.[3]

No One Has Ever Seen God and Lived

Whatever human words may be used to penetrate somewhat the inner mystery of God's nature as love in a communion of persons, our attitude demands something of the apophatic approach of the early Eastern Fathers. We must realize that we cannot comprehend God's inner life completely or we would have to be part of that Godly family by our very nature.

Yet scripture insists that we can know this God-Trinity by not knowing him. In our poverty and utter creatureliness, in our sinfulness and alienation from the Father, we realize that to know God is beyond our power. "No one has ever seen God. It is God the only Son, who is close to the Father's heart, who has made him known" (John 1:18).

God Manifests Himself to Us through His Word

The Johannine Gospel powerfully speaks of God's eternal Word:

> In the beginning was the Word, and the Word was with God, and the Word was God. He was in the beginning with God. All things came into being through him... (John 1:1–2)

This Divine Word became flesh and "lived among us" (John 1:14). It is he, therefore, who can reveal to us that the Father is known to himself and to us in and through his very Word. "His name is called the Word of God" (Rev 19:13). St. Ignatius of Antioch describes how God manifests himself through his Word: "There is one God, who manifested himself through Jesus Christ his Son, who is his Word, proceeding from silence."[4]

This Word is the perfect image of the invisible God (Col 1:15). He is the thought of the Father that contains all the knowledge that the Father has of himself and of his eternal Son and of all things in that Word. "He is the reflection of God's glory and the exact imprint of God's very being..." (Heb 1:3).

Holy scripture teaches us in the words of Jesus that the Word of God receives all its force and power from the Father. He is the perfect reflection of the Mind that speaks this Word. "The Son can do nothing on his own, but only what he sees the Father doing, for whatever the Father does, the Son does likewise" (John 5:19).

The Only Son of God, Of One Substance with the Father

St. Athanasius of the fourth century used the Logos doctrine as the Image of the Father, having no immediate relationship to the created, in order to conclude that, therefore, he is like the Father in the same essence, as the Councils of Nicene (AD 325) and Constantinople (AD 381) affirmed. The term *Logos* had an appeal in the early Church for those educated in Greek philosophy. But the term *Son* was frequently applied to Jesus Christ by the faithful as well as by the Fathers of the Church. And this was so for two main reasons: first, Jesus himself both in the words of the New Testament and in the liturgy is referred to as the Son of God.

St. John presents the Son as the expressed love of the Father for us: "For God so loved the world that he gave his only Son…in order that the world might be saved through him" (John 3:16–17; also John 4:9). The Father is greater than the Son (John 14:28) since everything that the Son has, has come to him from the Father as from his Source. Jesus is in the Father and the Father is in him (John 14:10). Jesus told his disciples that, seeing him, they would see also the Father.

Jesus revealed to us the intimate relationships between his Father and himself. The doctrine of grace would be culled from the Last Supper Discourses in John 14–17 from such revelation. We can see how most important it is to ground ourselves on this basic revelation of the Trinity from scripture in order to extend those intratrinitarian relationships into our own divine filiation with the Father through the Son in his Spirit.

The Spirit of God

But if there were only the Father and the Son, there would be no community of two Persons giving themselves to each other and fructifying in a third. There would be no movement outside of a mutual desire toward "union." The result would be not only a denial of the Trinity but also a negation of a God who has so loved us as to give us his only begotten Son so that in his gift, the Spirit of Love, we may have eternal life (John 3:16).

As we quoted from Richard of St. Victor, true love is driven to a transcendence that wishes love received to be shared by a third person. He argues for the existence within the Trinity of the Holy Spirit on the basis of the psychology of love. The Son wants to love the Father with a perfect mutual love just as the Father loves him.

According to Richard, it would be an imperfection between the Father and the Son if their love did not want to be shared with another. But to share this mutual love, there is need of a *"condilectum,"* one that is loved equally as the Father loves the Son and the Son loves the Father. This is the Holy Spirit.

The Holy Spirit Unites the Father and the Son

If the Father and the Son mutually know themselves, this is brought about necessarily by the Holy Spirit who allows them, not only mutually to affirm themselves as Father and Son, but also mutually to recognize themselves as such. The Father and Son, knowing themselves in that primal act of the "emptying" of the Father into the Son and the Son's "emptying" of himself into the Father in mutual self-surrender is nothing but the binding force of the Holy Spirit as love.

Thus the Holy Spirit cannot be an accidental relation, a "thing" produced, even from all eternity; but in a mysterious manner the Holy Spirit unites the Father and Son eternally in love that cannot be separated from the knowing by the Father in his Son. The Spirit makes it possible that the unity of the Godhead can be still shared without destroying that unity in the diversity of Persons, who share in that essence.

From this threefold movement flows, therefore, all reality within the Trinity and without, that is, in the order of creation, and God's shared being through his uncreated energies of love. The Divine Logos is the natural and perfect expression of the Father and is naturally and perfectly expressed by the love of the Father, that is, the Spirit.

Knowledge is not enough, but it must be completed by love in freedom since it exists in that first movement of self-giving. Love completes the knowledge and, although knowledge and love are not the same, within the Trinity both the Son as known in the love of the Father and as knowing the Father in his returned love can be possible only through realized love, which is the Spirit, proceeding from the Father along with the Son. Yet both proceed differently from the one Source.

An Unchanging Movement

This eternal movement within the Trinity is totally an immanent action that knows no finite beginning, increase, or cessation. It is an eternal "insession" or, to use the word coined by the early Greek Fathers, a *"perichoresis."* It is a relational interpenetration of all three Persons, distinct by their oppositional relationships. Yet all are one in the very knowing and loving that each possesses the same nature.

This "perichoresis" in knowledge and love, in unity and distinction, is the basis for God's trinitarian "interpenetration" within us human beings as the trinitarian indwelling, as will be developed later. God's sharing his being with us human beings is to be found in his "homely" love, to quote Julian of Norwich (fourteenth-century English anchorite mystic). This "homely" love is God calling us into his very own family, God's "home." To make his home with us is to take us into his very own "family." He allows us to participate in his divine nature as 2 Peter 1:4 says.

Within the Trinity, therefore, because of God's divine, perfect love in wanting to know and love himself in his Son and Spirit, we find the basis of all reality. Love becomes energized love when it is an actualized sharing of one's being with another. True love always is rooted in self-giving to another and thus the "Self-Giver" finds his uniqueness distinct from the other, yet in perfect unity.

If Jesus Christ, the Word of God incarnate and the perfect image of the Heavenly Father in human form, became that perfect expression of the Father's love both for himself and for all of us loved by the Father in his Word, then we can understand how Christ's *kenosis,* or total self-emptying of himself on the cross, tells us something of the Father's self-giving within the Trinity. This is the basis of all true self-giving and the energies of love, primal grace, that make all human loves and self-givings possible. Now we are able to reflect on the unique personhood of the Son and that of the Holy Spirit within the Trinity, the circle of Divine Love that knows no circumference.

CHAPTER FOUR

The Holy Spirit in the Trinity

When Pope Paul VI concluded the Ecumenical Council of Vatican II in 1965, he invited all the observers from the various Eastern Churches, the Anglican Church, and all the invited Protestant participants. He cordially thanked them for their presence and then asked them what helpful criticism would they wish to point out to him. Almost to a person, they unanimously criticized the Catholic speakers and the various *periti* (experts) who had worked so diligently over three years formulating a huge number of documents: why did they forget the Holy Spirit?

Pope Paul VI gratefully thanked them and resolved that the leaders of the Roman Catholic Church would surely work on this most important theme of the Holy Spirit in future gatherings of bishops in upcoming synods. Pope John Paul II as well often expressed the urgent need to study the role and importance of the Holy Spirit within the Roman Church.

Who Is the Holy Spirit?

Of the three Persons of the Trinity, the Holy Spirit seems to most Christians to be the most "impersonal" and mysterious, the one who is most difficult for us to imagine with our mental concepts or to relate to from our own human relationships. All three Divine Persons are spirits and are invisible to us. Yet we do somehow or other relate to the Son and the Father since such mutual relationships between our own earthly fathers and our own "sonships" or "daughterships" are experiential and can give us a human knowledge that presents us with real elements in the nature of the Divine Father and the only begotten Son of the Father.

A God Separated from His Creation

One reason why we Christians make up a very dysfunctional Church has been the vision over the centuries of separating our Christian faith from the scientific, material world around us. Our spiritual life was concerned with God's revelation about himself in his inner nature as Trinity and in his extrinsic relations to us human beings. God revealed the invisible world of heaven that would await us beyond this perishable, material world that all too often was regarded as an obstacle to the spiritual life. Our ascetical efforts to develop Christian virtues were looked upon as a way of accumulating graces in order to merit a high reward in heaven.

The Trinity Relates to the World

If we truly believe that the same Father, Son, and Spirit—who dwell within their eternal community, within us individuals, and within the Church—dwell also in their material world as in a sacred temple, then we must be guided by the threefold presence of the Trinity to the world.

First, from scripture both in the Old and New Testaments we believe that the entire, created universe comes from God and is being sustained by the actively involved Trinity as creation is being uttered by the Godhead into being by his Word and the Holy Spirit. The Trinity of one divine, loving nature is constantly calling into greater being this universe toward a loving unity by the creative Spirit of God's love.

The Holy Spirit Unveils to Us
The Trinity's Loving Activities in the Cosmos

Second, the universe is destined by the Trinity to be guided toward the Trinity as its goal, since the whole cosmos is an immense symbol of the Trinity's revelation to us. Science and religion, when united and not separated from each other, make possible the highest, most transcendent religious experiences of the Trinity. We Christians are especially called through infused faith, hope, and love by the Holy Spirit to discover the Trinity's active presence within all of creation. We are invited to work in a "synergism," a working together to bring all of God's creation into full completion through the Father, Son, and Spirit.

Third, more specifically, as we discover the immanent Trinity within the historical world of the present, we also discern that it has been the same Trinity as has been working in the historical past up to the present time. We Christians are to live and creatively work according to the Spirit's gifts given each of us for a variety of purposes to bring about a greater refulgence of the Trinity in and through the universe.

Stress on Interpersonal Relations

Today among Western philosophers and theologians, there is a great emphasis on interpersonal relationships. Heribert Mühlen, SJ, has brought about an exciting synthesis of the insights of past theologians, such as Augustine, Richard of St. Victor, Thomas Aquinas, and Duns Scotus, to highlight the interpersonal relationships within the Trinity.[1]

Mühlen takes many insights from the metaphysics of language as explored by Dietrich von Hildebrand[2] and Wilhelm von Humboldt[3] in order to show the distinctive personality of the Holy Spirit as coming out of an I-Thou relationship between Father and Son within the Trinity.

When we seek to probe more deeply the meaning of the Holy Spirit, both within the Trinity and within our own spiritual life, we find many difficulties. Historically, in the great ecumenical councils, the dogma about the divinity of the Holy Spirit and his relationship with the Father and the Son had been articulated only after the great christological dogmas had been clarified. This is no doubt due to the lack of clarity found in holy scripture. But it also means that a doctrine that depends totally upon other doctrines cannot be clarified until such prior doctrines have been clearly enunciated. The implications of the Holy Spirit could have been drawn only when the full divinity of the Son—of the same nature as the Father, an equal I-Thou-Community—was firmly established.

An I-Thou-We-Community

However, the greatest deterrent in presenting the Holy Spirit as the transforming love of the Father and the Son that divinizes us into the very community of the Trinity came through the scholastic presentation both of the Holy Spirit and the Trinity. The four Aristotelian categories to explain any causality (that is, material, formal, efficient, and final causes) were used by the medieval Scholastic theologians to explain both the actions of the Trinity outside of itself toward the created world and also to describe the operations of the individual Persons indwelling us through created grace.

Created grace, as habitual and sanctifying, was objectivized away from the personal love relationships of the trinitarian Persons toward us. Mühlen helps us to recapture the insights of holy scripture, especially the *hesed* covenant. He also allows us to interpret grace primarily, as the early Greek Fathers did, as the "uncreated energies" of the total God-Community, meeting us individuals with the individuated, personalized relationships of each trinitarian Person as found within the Trinity-Community.

Using the insight of von Humboldt,[4] that speech can arise only through the mediation of a duality. We have already pointed out how the Father knows himself in his Word and Son, and the Son knows himself only in the Father. It is the Holy Spirit, who then brings about a We-relationship. Dietrich von Hildebrand explains how the We-relationship builds upon the I-Thou as the foundation, making a third in a "common performance of acts and attitudes."[5]

The Father not only knows himself in his Son, but he also acknowledges himself as uniquely the Son's Father. The opposition between the Father and Son only increases the intimacy the more each Person acknowledges both his own uniqueness and also that of the Other. Teilhard de Chardin declares that "love differentiates as it unites."[6] As the uniqueness of each person increases the intimacy and the desire for greater union, love is generated and brings about the union.

The Personalized Act of Love: The Holy Spirit

This love within the Trinity cannot be a created "thing." It must be the personalized Act of Love, coming out of the mutual love of the Father and Son, loving each other in "our

Spirit." The Spirit "proceeds" from the union of the two, uniquely different Persons, Father and Son. The Holy Spirit's being as a Person within the Trinity consists of being the act of union and distinction between the Father and Son, and in this "action," the Spirit discovers his "personality." Thus the Holy Spirit can never be considered apart from either the Father or the Son.

The Filioque Controversy

Speaking the Word in eternal silence through his outpouring love that is his Holy Spirit, the Heavenly Father hears his Word come back to him in a perfect, eternal "yes" of total surrendering love that is again the Holy Spirit.

The theological controversy between the Orthodox and the Catholic Churches about the *"Filioque"* (that is, whether the Holy Spirit proceeds from the Father alone or also from the Son)[7] need not be a controversy when this teaching is contemplated in the eternal begetting of God's Word in God's Love. Both Churches hold a partial statement of the truth. The contemplative, who stands before this sacred mystery, knows from a knowledge given only by God's Spirit that the Holy Spirit proceeds as the Gift of Love from the Father, and in this same proceeding Act of Love the Word is eternally spoken, known, and loved. But the Son echoes, or as the Orthodox teach, radiates the Holy Spirit, as the Word goes back to the Father in the same Divine Spirit of Love.

The Spirit originates from the Father, but through the mediation of the Son, who forms with the Father the I-Thou community, and through the Spirit, the Trinity becomes a We-Community. The Spirit also proceeds back to the Father as the Word's loving response. The Holy Spirit is the silent gasp of mutual, loving surrender between the Father and the Son. The Holy Spirit brings to completion the divine union between the Father and Son in the ecstasy of shared love.

The Spirit of Unity and Distinction

Thus we discover the Holy Spirit, not as a separated entity within the Trinity, but in his personhood, in the light of the unity and distinction between the Father and the Son through the Spirit's bringing-about, through mutual love, the union of the Father and the Son and their uniqueness of differentiated Persons in the We-Community. It is therefore within the Trinity that we must first contemplate the activities of the Holy Spirit as the gift of bonding love between the Father and Son.[8] For the very gift of God's Spirit to us is the gift that "goes forth" in self-emptying love from the Father to the Son. The true nature of love is to be experienced in the self-gifting between two persons.

No image, no word, no symbol, no sign can truly capture the Holy Spirit and declare: "Here we have captured God's Spirit! He is here and not there. He is this and not that." Like Moses, we are to approach the burning bush, take off our shoes, and fall down in adoration to be enlightened by the invisible Spirit of God, who is always operating as loving activity in every facet of God's created world. His works of love are visible and experienced only in our intimate oneness with him as we purify ourselves of our own deluded power and no longer know the Holy Spirit as an object. In utter emptiness of heart we wait for the wind, the fire, the living waters to rush upon us and reveal himself in his loving activities in bringing about the union of the Father and Son in the We-Community of the Trinity in the uniqueness of the three Persons as they share their very same divine nature that is always LOVE. Now we can reflect on God's revelation of his holiness as it stretches down to engulf us also into their We-Community through the Body of Christ in his Spirit, who makes of us with our cooperation his very own Temple through the indwelling Trinity—Father, Son, Spirit within us.

Chapter Five

The Mystery of the Incarnation

A poem written in Sanskrit five thousand years ago recalls to us anxious modern women and men that joyful childself we have locked deep in the labyrinth of our unconscious. In embryonic form, that little child beckons us grown-up human beings into a newness of life, possible only if it were to let these powers unfold from within us:

> See yourself bestowing your goodness and warmth to all.
> Call upon the forces of good to pervade all things.
> Reach out beyond knowing and embrace oneness.
> Healing as you go, breathe the living word restoring creation.
> Share the spiritual fire and let the mystic light of God fill you to overflowing.
> Ultimately there is only one truth, one pure blessed reality:
> That the powers of love will pervade and overcome all things.
> We will rest in utter completion of wonder.
> We are not alone, but we are within the same mystical unfolding.
> Happy are we only in as far as kindness and vision live within, shining outward.

> Words are shadows; acts are born of real caring and loving.
> A truth in stillness do we share in the moments beyond time,
> Fleeting touches of an ultimate total embrace.
> Within these things lies the most sacred and simple mystery of all:
> We are loved, utterly and completely.[1]

The First Man and Woman

The first human beings were created as mystics, at home in heaven and on earth, drawing no line between the two. They took in the unified field of nature and spirit in one visionary glance and drank living water from the well of that Absolute Being we now call God. Because they in the beginning did not separate themselves from God or God from the world, they looked at creation and agreed with God that it was good. After the joyful harvest of their days, they danced, then slept, and danced again, to the endless music of their dreams.

Such a being it was that Jesus took on his lap and held in his arms, saying, "Unless you change and become like children, you will never enter the kingdom of heaven" (Matt 18:3).

The Meaning of Human Sin

Adam and Eve lost this childhood and became fragmented and separated from God and from each other. They recognized in shame and guilt that they disobeyed God's loving commands; God was no longer the Ultimate Source for them as they measured all creatures only by their own self-centered desires.

Noble humankind was created by God-Trinity to be made in God's image, according to his likeness (Gen 1:26–27) and to be "...a little lower than God" (Ps 8:5). We become a quintessence of dust as we build up bigger walls to separate ourselves from others. We learned down through the history of mankind to put on masks and play roles before each other, hollow persons who speak in hollow voices, stuffed with the straw of our ego, our bones too dry to live. Anxieties and fears increase as we continue to be false to those true selves that might rise like living water from God within us.

We Created an Unreal World in Our Minds

We now live in a false world that we continually create within ourselves and show on the movie screen of our own minds. No one except us comes to this interior theater, but we hardly notice, so in love are we with our own false images and their creator, ourselves. In every movie we play the hero, refusing to see that we are also the villain.

We fear God's terrifying punishment, God's self-revelation as utterly different from our poor selves, and so we hide, not as Adam and Eve hid behind fig leaves in their nakedness, but behind the masks and games that separate us from the world around us.

...And the Word Became Flesh

The mystery of the Incarnation reveals to us through the materiality of the human nature of Christ what our own humanity can attain by God's grace. This dogma of the hypostatic union teaches us that the Second Person of the Trinity, who operates equally and conjointly with the other two Persons in all their divine energies of love, acting throughout the universe, now assumes a human nature like our own.

St. Paul beautifully describes how great the trinitarian community loves us in the mystery of Jesus' Incarnation:

> Though he was in the form of God,
> did not regard equality with God
> as something to be exploited,
> but emptied himself,
> taking the form of a slave,
> being born in human likeness.
> And being found in human form,
> he humbled himself
> and became obedient to the point of death—
> even death on a cross. (Phil 2:6–8)

Importance of the Incarnation for Us

We would always have been unable to enter into "personalized" relations with the Father, different from those of the Son and Holy Spirit, if it had not been for the Incarnation. The eternal Word made flesh is able by the Incarnation to act in the historical, horizontal level in a unique manner that reflected somewhat his very own oppositional relationships to the Father and the Holy Spirit within the immanent life of the Trinity.

When Christ assumed a human nature like unto our own, we learn from the author of the Epistle to the Hebrews: "For we do not have a high priest who is unable to sympathize with our weaknesses, but we have one who in every respect has been tested as we are, yet without sin. Let us therefore approach the throne of grace with boldness, so that we may receive mercy and find grace to help in time of need" (Heb 4:15–16).

Christ's human nature did not exist of itself and then was merely added somehow to the Divine Word. In that very act the Word, preexistent from all eternity, gave existence to his human nature and divinized it.

Jesus Christ: The *Pontifex Maximus*

This humanity had the immortal and incorruptible character of the nature of Adam before he sinned; yet Jesus Christ in his humanity was subjected to the conditions of our own fallen natures, as St. Maximus the Confessor (d. 662) writes.[2] For him, Christ is the *"Pontifex Maximus,"* the greatest of all bridge-builders, who spans the infinite world of God (including the personalized world of the three Persons) and the finite world of mankind and all created beings.

St. Maximus writes:

> We are astonished to see how the finite and the infinite things which exclude one another and cannot be mixed are found to be united in him and are manifested mutually the one in the other. For the unlimited is limited in an ineffable manner, while the limited is stretched to the measure of the unlimited.[3]

All Creatures Are Created In and For the Logos

The Second Person as Logos has been revealing the hidden Godhead from the beginning of creation with a personalized act different from the Father. The Father and Source of all being creates all created world in and through his Word by the overshadowing of his Spirit of Love: "All that came to be had life in him (the Logos)..." (John 1:3).

But through the Incarnation, the Second Person continues now through the humanity assumed by the Logos to reveal himself to us through specific actions reflecting that immanent action of the Son within the Trinity. The human nature of Christ is totally penetrated by the one divine nature. It is "existentially" united to the Second Person of the Trinity and not to the First, the Father, nor to the Third, the Holy Spirit.

Theosis: Sharers of God's Nature

St. Athanasius (d. 371) succinctly summarizes the end of the Incarnation:

> The Divine Word was made man that we might become gods. He was made visible through his body in order that we might have an idea of the invisible Father (Col 1:15). He has supported the outrages of men in order that we may have a part of his immortality.[4]

As the Heavenly Father eternally begets his Son, so in the historical salvific order, in the life of Jesus Christ, and in a parallel way in our own lives, that same Father is begetting his Son, Jesus Christ; and through him and his Holy Spirit, he is begetting us in his Son to be his adopted children. St. Cyril of Alexandria (d. 444) explains the importance of the Incarnation to restore our filiation to God the Father, which was lost by Adam and Eve:

> By the Incarnation we also—in him and through him, according to nature and grace—have been made sons of God; according to nature insofar as we are one in him (through the same human nature), by participation and according to grace through himself in the Spirit.[5]

The End of Our Earthly Life

The end of our lives is to grow continually into an ever-increasing awareness of oneness in Christ Jesus. This is what we read in the Second Epistle of Peter: "Thus he has given us, through these things, his precious and very great promises, so that through them you may escape from the corruption that is in the world because of lust, and may become participants of the divine nature" (2 Pet 1:4).

God Allures Us to Share in the Divine Nature by Christ's Humanity

This is what the Greek Fathers mean by "divinization" (*theosis* in Greek).[6] We are to live in the "likeness" of Jesus Christ; that is, to share in his very own life made possible by the Holy Spirit. St. Bernard preached that God entices us to love him by giving us the humanity of his Son as the point of attraction.

Jesus Christ images the divinity of God that radiates through the frailness and lowliness of his humanity. His meekness and gentleness draw us without any threatening fear to surrender to his Spirit. The glory or power of God in his Word radiates in the teachings, miracles, and healings of Jesus in scripture. It is through Jesus of Nazareth, who died and was raised up from the dead, that all of God's grace and glory will be given to us to share with him his divine nature. "No one has ever seen God. It is God the only Son, who is close to the Father's heart, who has made him known" (John 1:18).

The Gift of Divinization Is Only from God

Since our human divinization is the result of the hypostatic unity between the divine and human natures in Christ,

St. Maximus over and over insists that such a divinization of human beings could never be the result of powers within the God-given creation of our human nature.[7]

Jesus Christ perfectly and faithfully represents his Father to us in human communication of words and actions. When he loves us, especially by freely dying for us on the cross, we can experience the love of the Father. "As the Father has loved me, so I have loved you" (John 15:9). Everything Jesus says or does is the Word of God. He can do nothing but what the Father tells him to do.

Yet only Jesus Christ, the Second Person of the Trinity in his human nature, goes to his death. Through Christ's hypostatic union, he is fully human in his human *nature,* with a human will, yet through being the Father's eternal and only begotten Son, his only *person* is that of the Second Person, the Son of the Father. Thus we can declare that Mary, Jesus' mother, gave birth (*theotokos* in Greek: the birth-giver) to the total Person we call Jesus Christ, the one Person who died on our behalf. If Jesus also had, not only a full human nature, but also a human *person,* then it would have been his human person that died for us. This is the condemned heresy of Nestorianism of the fifth century in the Council of Ephesus (431). No human person would have the power to reconcile us to the Heavenly Father.

We Are Saved Through the Death of Christ

Paul saw clearly that we have been reconciled only because Jesus Christ who died for us is the only begotten Son of the Heavenly Father. Paul writes:

> Indeed, rarely will anyone die for a righteous person—though perhaps for a good person someone might actually dare to die. But God proves his love

for us in that while we still were sinners Christ died
for us....For if while we were enemies, we were reconciled to God through the death of his Son, much
more surely, having been reconciled, will we be saved
by his life. (Rom 5:7–10)

Jesus Is the Image of the Unseen God

Jesus is God from God, Light from Light. Who sees him sees the Father who is imaged in Jesus' words and his human actions, especially in his kenotic death on the cross.

He is the image of the invisible God, the firstborn of all creation; for in him all things in heaven and on earth were created, things visible and invisible, whether thrones or dominions or rulers or powers—all things have been created through him and for him. He himself is before all things, and in him all things hold together. He is the head of the body, the church; he is the beginning, the firstborn from the dead, so that he might come to have first place in everything. (Col 1:15–19)

The Father begets his Son through the overshadowing of the Spirit, as Luke records in Luke 1:35. The Father continues acting his personalized role as Begetter in our own divinization through his Son and the Holy Spirit.

The Role of the Holy Spirit

The goal of our human existence is to be divinized through the personalized actions of the Father, Son, and Holy Spirit into a likeness to the Son of God in the Holy Spirit. It is a process of becoming as God is: a We-Community that is personalized Love in a oneness of nature and in uniqueness of persons. As both the Son and the Holy Spirit "proceed" from the Father as from their Source, so they cannot be separated in their salvific actions that, nevertheless, are distinctive to each Person.

Because the Holy Spirit is "hypostasized" Love, binding the Father and Son together, some modern Orthodox theologians like to describe the work of the Holy Spirit in terms of a *kenosis* (a Greek word meaning an emptying out in perfect love. Cf. Phil 2:6–9). This is the characteristic of trinitarian, personalized love. Though Christ is even now in glory, his self-emptying until the last drop of blood and water on the cross (John 19:34–45) goes on, due to the humanity that links him with all of us human beings.

The Spirit Is Personified Holiness Reflecting the Essence of Divine Love

But the *kenosis* of the Holy Spirit is a constant, hidden giving of the Father and Son to us that persists from Pentecost until the Parousia in this economy of salvation.[8] The personhood of the Holy Spirit is hidden in a personalized self-emptying that characterizes Love itself. He is personified Holiness because he reflects the essence of divine holiness. The holiness of God is seen as triune Love in the Holy Spirit that Sergé Bulgakov called "hypostatic Love."

We Share God's Eternal Life Through the Gift of the Holy Spirit

The Holy Spirit is both the Giver and the Gift of life (John 6:63). He gives divine life to us through Jesus Christ, but he is also the Father's Gift to us through Jesus. All we have to do is to ask for this Gift and the Father will give us a share in him (Luke 11:13). Jesus describes the Holy Spirit as the Advocate *(Parakletos):* "When the Advocate comes, whom I will send to you from the Father, the Spirit of truth who comes from the Father, he will testify on my behalf" (John 15:26).

Entering into the Kingdom of God

The Holy Spirit gives us himself as the Gift of Love from the Father and the Son, thus leading us into the kingdom of God. To seek the kingdom of God is to seek the Holy Spirit for he pours into our hearts all the gifts necessary to enter into a living relationship as a renewed child of God the Father. Paul emphatically writes:

> For all who are led by the Spirit of God are children of God. For you did not receive a spirit of slavery to fall back into fear, but you have received a spirit of adoption. When we cry, "Abba! Father!" it is that very Spirit bearing witness with our spirit that we are children of God. (Rom 8:14–17)

Submission to the Holy Spirit

The personality and work of the Holy Spirit can be seen only in the light of the personality and work of the Father and the Son. The Spirit is present in the eternal birth of the Son. So also he realizes the conception of the Son in history in the womb of Mary.

So likewise the Spirit effects our own being, begotten of the Father through the Son. Jesus in his lifetime was submissive to the Spirit. All of his acts—his performing miracles, his healings, his forgiving of sins, his driving out of demons, and especially his surrendering of his very own life into the hands of his Heavenly Father—were all performed by the action of the Spirit within the heart of Jesus. So we find our fullness as human beings by being submissive to the Holy Spirit.

The work of Jesus and the Spirit in the Incarnation, in redemption, and in Pentecost through the Church of Jesus is climaxed in the goal of the mutual cooperation of Jesus and the Spirit to divinize us into the children of the Heavenly Father.

Neither Person in the Trinity is more important, nor does one do more than the others. They "co-serve" each other to "recapitulate" or to bring to completion the Father's eternal plan of creating us and sharing his divine life through his Son incarnate through the Spirit of Love.

The Completion of the Father's Eternal Plan of Salvation

As the Spirit brings the Father and Son together into a loving community and brings about in that mutual love a union of love and a self-knowledge in self-giving to each other, so the same Spirit brings us, many brothers and sisters, into the one begotten Son, Jesus Christ, and constitutes the Body of Christ, the Church.

We have focused in this chapter on the importance of the mystery of the Incarnation. We have seen from the New Testament's teaching of the Word made flesh, Jesus Christ, why he took upon himself our human nature: "Yes, God loved the world so much that he gave his only Son, so that everyone who believes in him may not be lost but may have eternal life" (John 3:16).

Grace is God loving his human creation and deifying it through his activities with human beings, who freely choose

Jesus Christ as the Way that leads to the Truth that leads to Life (John 14:6), which is Love Personified.

Through the doctrine of God's energies of love, the Trinity, as through the Incarnation, is now seen as "God for us." We can solve the antinomy between a God who cannot in any way be comprehended in his divine nature or essence and a God who is constantly communicating himself to us through the Word incarnated.

Chapter Six

God's Exploding Love

In this chapter I would like to explore the important distinction of the early Greek Fathers between God's awesome majesty and perfect, infinite essence or divine nature, and God's uncreated energies of love. Western Christians need to study how these great and holy theologians maintained in happy tension the infinite transcendence of an infinitely perfect God with the revealed truth by Jesus Christ of the immanence of a triune, loving community. This trinitarian community seeks to divinize us through their indwelling presence within us. Our very brokenness and inner poverty of spirit prepare us for such a mystical oneness with God-Trinity within us.

The Unapproachable One

In such brokenness, the Christian should know that God is unreachable and unknowable by human power alone. Yet no matter how poor and empty we know ourselves to be, we do begin to feel God's infilling come upon us. God "...is not far from each one of us. For in him we live and move and have our being" (Acts 17:28).

Eastern Christian theologians from earliest time appealed to holy scripture to substantiate their teachings on the distinction between God's infinite essence and his energies. St. Basil of the fourth century insisted: "It is by God's energies that we say we know our God. We do not assert that we can come near to his essence itself, for his energies descend to us, but his essence remains unapproachable."[1]

Basil shows how the unapproachable and unknowable essence of God can, however, be experienced through the uncreated energies of the divine nature:

> If it were possible to contemplate the divine nature itself in itself and find out what is proper to it and what is foreign through what appears, we would be in no need at all of words or other signs for the comprehension of what is sought. But because it is higher than the understanding of the things sought...it is of all necessity that we be conducted by the "energies" to the research of the divine nature.[2]

The Forthgoing of God

What St. Gregory Palamas of the fourteenth century would call simply God's "energy"—following the term used by the Cappadocian Fathers Basil, Gregory Nazianzus, and Gregory Nyssa of the fourth century—the great unknown Pseudo-Dionysius of the latter part of the fifth century would call by various attributes, showing how God goes forth toward his created world to share his being or unlimited perfections.

Some of the Areopagite's expressions indicating God's energies are the following: God's "forthgoing" (*"proodos"* in Greek), the manifestation of God's light or the divine "illumination" or the ray *("aktina")* of God as the "supersubstantial ray," and finally the "distribution."

Mystical Union

Dionysius stresses that the goal of our human lives is to attain "mystical knowledge," the summit of God's sharing himself with us. This is brought about by God's "energetic actions" toward us, which the Areopagite author insists as completely gratuitous on God's part. It is not we who raise ourselves to such a mystical union, but God's freely given energies, which work in us.

This mystical union with the Trinity is a mystery. How can God share the divine nature with us in such a way that we really participate in God's divinity without, at the same time, becoming God? This is the mystery of *theosis,* a word Dionysius took from the writings of the third-century Clement of Alexandria. This is what would be translated by the terms "deification" or "divinization" to describe the process of grace whereby Christians are brought into a loving union with God through the uncreated, divine energies, and still God retains his complete superessential being.

Part of this mystery of how individuals really do experience the full divinity, and yet each individual experiences God in his energies according to different proportions, is stated in Dionysius' expression: "It is all the divinity completely which is participated by each participator, and by none in any part."[4]

Knowledge in a God-Fitting Manner

To maintain such an antinomy Dionysius gives us a principle taken from one of his favorite theological sources, Gregory Nazianzus: "Divine things should be understood in a God-fitting manner."[5]

It is this which theologians must ever keep in mind that alone will resolve all apparent contradictions and justify all antinomies in divine matters. No distinction humanly made can adequately describe the distinction between God's simplicity and essence and his participable self-giving in his energies.

The Nature of the Divine Energies

The energies are manifestations of God. Still, even though they are many and diverse, they are "one" in God. Hence, God's simplicity is maintained, but not at the price of isolating him from contact with his creation. These manifestations are "God coming forth," that is, God insofar as he does not hide in his unknowable essence, but reveals himself to us human beings.[6]

St. Gregory Palamas (1296–1359), Archbishop of Thessalonica, has given the Greek Orthodox Church the most thorough teaching on the distinction between God's transcendent Divine Nature, incomprehensible to all human beings, and God's uncreated energies that make the indwelling Trinity possible so the justified persons can be deified by grace and "become participants of the divine nature" (2 Pet 1:4), without ever becoming God. His teachings were confirmed by the Greek councils held in Constantinople in 1341 and 1351.

The Face of God

Archbishop Joseph Raya beautifully summarizes Palamas' doctrine in his book *The Face of God:*

> It is not God's action, but God himself in his actions, who makes himself known to human persons and gives them the ability to "see" him. God enters into the love of holy persons and remains here in his intimate reality. The presence is real; indeed, most real. This communication of God is not "things," which

exist outside of God; not "gifts" of God. They are God himself in his action. They are the very God, who is himself Uncreated. They are, therefore, called "uncreated" because their cause and origin are the Essence of God. In them God, as it were, goes beyond himself and becomes "trans-radiant" in order to really communicate himself. Thus the Essence and energies of God are not "parts" of God, but two ways by which we human beings can contemplate God's essence.[7]

God's Uncreated Energies: God for Us

The energies of God are, we might say, "God for us." They are God in loving and creative relationship to us out of the motive of sharing his holiness and inner life with us. Palamas introduces a distinction that is important in the history of the theology of God's knowability. God for us is *"Theos,"* whereas God in himself is *"Hyper-Theos."*[8] We can see again how both the communicability and the incommunicability of God are preserved.

Palamas even speaks of the "two sides" of God: higher and lower, superior and inferior.[9] However, in thus distinguishing the two aspects of "God *in se*" and "God for us," Palamas is not introducing a dichotomy into God, as if there were "two Gods." Rather, he is simply distinguishing the knowable from the unknowable in God.

Human Participation in God's Energies

Palamas, as we have seen above, works out a doctrine of God's essence and his uncreated energies in order to preserve the basic truth of Christian revelation, that all human beings have been in God's eternal love ordered to participate in his very own divine being (2 Pet 1:4).

These eternal energies are the thoughts of God, who is present in each of them. They are not, however, the essence of God. God is a living God, who is at the same time transcendent in his essence, but ever remains active through his energies. For Eastern Christian thought, the energies signify an exterior manifestation of the Trinity.

When God is described as love, life, and truth, and so on, we understand the energies as subsequent to the very being of the Trinity.

The Basis of All Christian Mysticism

The doctrine of the energies, as distinct from the essence, is the basis of all Christian mystical experience. God, who is inaccessible in his essence, is present in his energies "as a mirror," according to Palamas. God is wholly unknowable in his nature or essence, yet he is revealed in his energies.

This doctrine makes it possible to understand how the Trinity can remain incommunicable in essence, and yet dwell within us according to the promise of Christ. When one receives the deifying energies, one receives the indwelling of the Holy Trinity, which is inseparable from its natural energies.

Sharing God's Own Divine Nature

The distinction made between the essence and energies makes it possible to preserve the real meaning of the words "participants of the divine nature" (2 Pet 1:4). In deification or divinization, we are by grace what God is by nature, except that we remain creatures. Palamas explains this: "You do not however consider that God lets himself to be seen in his superessential essence, but according to the grace of adoption, uncreated deification and the direct hypostasized glory."[10]

The energies of God are uncreated divine activity. The divine essence, as we have repeatedly said above, is inaccessible. God, however, does communicate himself. He can be known experientially, and we can reach him in union or deification, that is, participating in God's own divine nature (2 Pet 1:4). Thus, this is a statement rooted solidly in the New Testament and the early Fathers of the Church, that God is both totally inaccessible in his divine essence and yet in his energies of divine love toward us is at the same time accessible.

Personalized Energies

For Palamas the divine energies are real (although not material nor merely an intellectual concept), essential (that is, not an accident), and yet really distinct from the actual essence of the Godhead. To avoid introducing a "quaternity" of four Persons in God, Palamas insists on the energies being "enhypostaton," introducing the term used by Leontius of Byzantium in the sixth century as that which signifies what is possessed, used, and manifested by a person.[11]

Here we come to the essential point of Palamas' distinction between God's essence and his energies. He insists that the energy, which the great Eastern saints saw as the "Taboric Light," similar to what Peter, James, and John experienced in the transfiguration of Christ with Moses and Elijah on Mount Tabor, is essentially personalized. Thus, this means that it is a common manifestation of the three Persons of the Trinity.

If this were not so, then God would be manifesting himself and divinizing human persons through an extrinsic grace, a created accident. The love relationship that allows God to share his very being and life with human beings would be only a moral arrangement and not a true regeneration of Christians into God's very own life, beginning in the sacraments, especially in baptism and above all in the Eucharist. In a word, God would not be really giving himself to us human beings, but he would be giving us a thing, different from the very own beings of the Holy Trinity in an extrinsic manner and not by direct contact with God's very own life.

Divine Grace

As did his predecessors, especially the Cappadocian Fathers, Palamas used the word *grace* in the many different ways found in the Greek language. He differentiates between "deifying grace" from the common uses of grace: "[T]he word 'grace' can designate the beauty, the beautiful appearance, the ornament and the glory of each nature, and in the sense we speak of the grace of words and of conversation....Hence there is a grace of nature different from deifying grace."[12]

In his letters against his adversary, Akindynos, Palamas denies the concept of a "created supernatural." "Primal grace" for him is God communicating, giving, manifesting himself to human beings: "There is a created grace and another grace uncreated....But since the gift which the saints receive and by which they are divinized is none other than God himself, how can you say that that is a created grace?"[13]

The Mystery of Our Cooperation

To make ourselves open to God's uncreated energies that are always "gracing" us at every moment in each event, we must enter into a "working with" God's gift of deifying grace that the Greek Fathers called a "synergy." All of us human beings are born into the original sin of Adam, yet we begin to leave "the pods that the pigs were eating" (Luke 15:16) in a *"metanoia"* or conversion and complete surrender to God's forgiving love.

When we cooperate with God's uncreated energies of love, the result is a divine state produced within the human soul. Palamas writes: "It is when you have in your soul the divine state that you really possess God within ourselves; and the true divine state is love toward God, and it survives only by practice of the divine commandments.[14]

Deification involves the union of divine and human wills. It is not something that simply happens to a person as from outside. We human beings must cooperate if God-Trinity can share with us in the depths of our souls. "Listen! I am standing at the door, knocking; if you hear my voice and open the door, I will come in to you and eat with you, and you with me" (Rev 3:20).

Knowing God in His Energies

Vladimir Lossky, one of the most representative theologians among the Orthodox of the twentieth century, describes divine grace in this way: "Grace signifies all the abundance of the divine nature, insofar as it is communicated to human beings,...the divine nature of which we partake through the uncreated energies."[15]

We can see how important this distinction is between God's essence as unknowable completely by us human beings and yet what we are able by the divine energies to experience as the indwelling Trinity. The Eastern Greek Fathers offer us in their doctrine of God's uncreated energies the foundation for the indwelling Trinity within the justified Christians, which is our prime focus in this book.

In Orthodox belief, intimate, direct communion with God-Trinity is the only means of human salvation, and such communion is what the divine energies as primal grace bring to the ardent followers of Christ. As we pointed out in this chapter, God in his uncreated energies of love is not simply a single, divine God, but an exploding, uncreated community of Trinity, Father, Son, and Holy Spirit who wish to unite us in loving union. This is the goal God has held out from all eternity, that the loving Trinity in their unity in diversity of persons wish us human beings to participate in their very divine nature and thus become the fulfillment of God's plan: "Let us make humankind in our image, according to our likeness" (Gen 1:26).

Is Grace Solely a Created Gift?

St. Thomas Aquinas of the thirteenth century, using Aristotle's categories, defines grace as the external principle of human actions: "Man needs a power added to his natural power by grace."[16] This he calls grace, a thing which God bestows upon a human person. Habitual grace justifies the soul or makes it acceptable to God. It is the infused, God-assisted habit of doing what God approves. Actual grace is the "supernatural" reality that God gives as a means of assistance.

Some modern Catholic theologians, such as Karl Rahner, warn against thinking of grace "materialistically." Grace is not a "'created,' sanctifying 'quality' produced in a 'recipient' in a merely causal way by God."[17] Rahner comes very close to describing the uncreated energies as grace in personalistic terms, similar to the Greek Fathers, when he writes:

Each one of the three divine persons communicates himself to man in gratuitous grace in his own personal particularity and diversity. This trinitarian communication is the ontological ground of man's life in grace and eventually of the direct vision of the divine persons in eternity.[18]

As long as grace is conceived of as solely a created entity, there cannot be an absolute mystery connected with it. If a created reality were substituted for God's self-communication, it would not be a communication of his Self. As Rahner says, "God would be the giver, not the gift itself ."[19]

Grounded upon Scripture and the Early Church Fathers

Grounded upon the scriptural and Greek patristic distinction between God's ineffable essence and his uncreated energies, we can maintain that God, in his essence as Trinity, is also the Giver and the Gift of the individuated Persons of the Trinity through the gift of uncreated grace personalized poured out into the adopted children of God as Uncreated Energies.

We are made by his energies through a union by grace with the indwelling Trinity to be participators in the divine nature, without, however, changing our human nature into the Divine. St. Symeon the New Theologian (949–1022) well summarizes this mystical union between the indwelling Trinity and the human children of God:

[T]he adoption through regeneration is due to the Holy Spirit, who makes us become gods by disposition and grace (*thesei kai chariti* in Greek) and who makes us to be heirs of God and co-heirs with

Christ...whereby we see God and himself living in us according to his divinity and moving around in a conscious *(gnostos)* manner within us.[20]

Contributions of Orthodox Theology

The greatest contribution from the Eastern Fathers for modern Western theology lies in their apophatic approach. This is seen in their distinction between the awesome transcendency of the Holy Trinity, unknowable through human rationality, and yet the personal union that comes about to justified Christians through the uncreated energies of God-Trinity whereby we can become sharers of God's divine nature without any hint of human beings becoming Gods. Perhaps Western theologians will more thoroughly study patristic theology, especially the theological anthropology of the early Greek Fathers of the Church, who developed a more scriptural, mystical, and personalistic relation between the Holy Trinity and the individual human being and even a cosmic transformation of all of God's created universe so that "Christ is all and in all" (Col 3:11).

The Eastern tradition offers fresh insights into the central truth of the Christian message that God condescends in his activities, especially through the God-Man, Jesus Christ, to make us into new creatures that will be the fulfillment of God's creating us according to the image and likeness of the God-Man by participating in God's divine nature. These insights could be a most important contribution to Western Christianity.

Such Eastern insights can keep before the Western mind, so gifted in logical thinking, this unique, ontological relationship between the Trinity and all human beings. A major contribution to the West may come through the Eastern concept of deification, seen as the holistic influence of primal grace as God's energies of love divinize the whole person "spirit and soul and body" (1 Thess 5:23).

A Holistic Spirituality

Palamas summarized the early Greek Fathers by cutting through the Platonizing tendency in much of Christian spirituality that interprets the Pauline categories of *flesh* and *spirit* as equivalents of the Platonic terms *matter* and *spirit* or *body* and *mind*. Palamas reinstates the categories in their correct Biblical form as referring to a human person without the trinitarian life and to the person graced by the Holy Spirit. Because all human beings are called to be opened to God's uncreated energies as primal grace on all levels, including our bodily relationships to God and the entire, created cosmos, Palamas considered us human beings as created superior even to the angels:

> Whereas the angels are appointed to serve the Creator and have as their only mission...while human beings are preordained, not only to be ruled, but to rule in and through Christ to bring the entire universe into the fullness according to the Logos in whom all things are created to be in Christ, for him and through him unto the total Trinity's full glory.[21]

Spiritualization of the Universe

Based on the writings of St. John and St. Paul, the Eastern approach has God divinizing Spirit-filled human beings, and then they, through their cooperation as active members of the Body of Christ, are guided by Christ and the Holy Spirit to reconcile the universe back to God. The influence of the

Johannine and Pauline writings in the New Testaments is evident in Paul's cosmic vision:

> So if anyone is in Christ, there is a new creation: everything old has passed away; see, everything has become new! All this is from God, who reconciled us to himself through Christ, and has given us the ministry of reconciliation; that is, in Christ God was reconciling the world to himself, not counting their trespasses against them, and entrusting the message of reconciliation to us. (2 Cor 5:17–19)

Profit for Eastern Theologians

We cannot be blinded to the fact that in the Eastern synthesis there are lacunae and deficiencies. Through the use of metaphors such as image, likeness, model, mirror, sun, and light rays, this whole Eastern doctrine—designed to explain the relation of God with finite human beings, the interrelation of nature and grace—can be dismissed as a lack of precision in speech and concept that may leave us with a seeming mere verbalism or at best beautiful poetry. The theology of the Eastern Fathers, therefore, can perhaps profit by being complemented in this doctrine of the uncreated energies and the image and likeness by the teachings of St. Augustine and St. Thomas. Both of these theologians of the West have also used the model of image and likeness in working out a theological anthropology.

Through much debating under the attacks of various heresies against grace, Augustine and Thomas were able to fashion concepts capable of clearly distinguishing the various points of relationship between nature in its different historical and possible stages, and grace, while all the time preserving God's gratuitous gift of grace and our human freedom to accept and to cooperate with God's uncreated energies of love.

Words of St. Gregory of Nyssa

These words of St. Gregory of Nyssa (d. 394) form a fitting close to this chapter. They speak the reverent mind of all the early Eastern Fathers as they contemplate what it means that God should so love us as to create us according to his image and likeness and surround us constantly with his loving energetic activities that are destined to divinize us into "real" children of God, if we would consent to live according to our God-given dignity:

> Man, who among beings counts for nothing, who is dust, grass, vanity, who was adopted to be a son of the God of the universe, becomes of this Being of such excellence and grandeur; this is a "mystery" that we can neither see nor understand nor comprehend. What thanks should man give for so great a favor? What word, what thought, what lifting up of mind in order to exalt the superabundance of this grace? Man surpasses his own very nature. From a mortal being, he becomes immortal, from a perishable being he becomes imperishable. From ephemeral he becomes eternal. In a word, from man he becomes god. In fact, rendered worthy to become a Son of God, he will have in himself the dignity of the Father. O munificence of the Lord, so bountiful....How great are the gifts of such ineffable treasures![22]

Chapter Seven

I Am the Vine–You Are the Branches

If your faith assures you that God is love and wishes to live most intimately within your very being, then what prevents you from experiencing this reality as a constant state? This reality is the end of the Incarnation, death, and resurrection of Jesus Christ. He came among us to make it possible, not only that we might become children of God, but that at all times we might also live consciously in that continued awareness discovered in each moment of our lives that the Trinity dwells within us.

This is your human dignity—to be called children of God—and you really are such children of God when in the process of discovering and surrendering to the uncreated energies of God living within you and within the context of each human situation or event. In substance, God is saying to you, "'Here I am.' Then he [says], 'Come no closer! Remove the sandals from your feet, for the place on which you are standing is holy ground'" (Exod 3:5).

Building a Loving Community

Christianity is a religion that builds a loving community, modeled on and empowered by the very intimate, loving, self-sacrificing community of the Trinity, Father, Son, and Holy Spirit. It is rooted in God, who wishes to communicate himself to us in the most intimate of unions. Holy scripture often uses the image of husband and wife to describe this tender relationship between God and ourselves. And we are to love one another as God, through Jesus, loves us in the Holy Spirit.

In Jesus' second farewell discourse in John's Gospel he uses allegory of the vine and the branches to convey, not only this great, intimate union between us individually and the indwelling Trinity, but also the necessity of our being united with him if we are to reach human fulfillment. Jesus insists that this fulfillment is to be measured by the love we have for others as we serve to build up the Christianity community of love, the total Christ, the Body and Head, the New Israel.

Vine/Vineyard History in Scripture

The agricultural image that Jesus uses meant much to his listeners in Palestine; it had a long, religious significance in the history of the Jewish people. The prophet Isaiah spoke of Israel as a vineyard planted by God with great effort, "but it yielded wild grapes" (Isa 5:2). God's word is even stronger through the prophet Jeremiah: "How then did you turn degenerate and became a wild vine?" (Jer 2:21). God spoke of the vine branches as useless and "given to the fire for fuel" to use the words of the prophet Ezekiel (Ezek 15:6). Thus, the vine was a symbol for Israel in the thinking of the Jews at the time of our Lord.[1]

Jesus: The True Vine

John builds upon the Old Testament and the Synoptic writings (Mark 12:1–12) to make Jesus the image of the true and only real (*alethinos* in Greek) living vine. The American Johannine scholar Raymond E. Brown says that the literary device of this allegory of the vine and the branches is more than the usual biblical forms of parables and allegory and fits the well-known form of the allegory called *mashal*.[2]

John the Evangelist uses this literary form of the *mashal* to describe several series of relationships of love *(agape)* uniting the Father and the Son, and disciples with Jesus and with one another: "I am the true vine, and my Father is the Vinedresser. Every branch of mine that bears no fruit, he takes away, and every branch that does bear fruit he prunes, that it may bear more fruit" (John 15:1–2).

The Father Prunes Us Out of Love for Us

Jesus insists not only on our union with him but also on the necessity that, as branches, we must be pruned by his Father, the Vinedresser, if we are to bring forth more fruit. Two activities are suggested as being works of the Vinedresser. The Father "removes every branch that bears no fruit [and every] branch that bears fruit he prunes to make it bear more fruit" (John 15:2–3).

Hearing God's Word Must Bring Forth Fruit

Jesus tells us that there are some branches that bear no fruit. They merely drain the vine of its energy. These are to be pruned away and burned. No doubt in this allegory Jesus was referring to the Jews who heard his words, but bore no fruit in building a loving community of the people of God. But Jesus also must have had in mind his future followers who would profess to be Christians and yet would never bring forth deeds of Christian love. These would also include the apostates down through the centuries who would refuse to listen to the teachings of Jesus given within his Body, the Church.

He is saying that unless those who have heard his words put them into practice with life-giving deeds of love, they will be fruitless branches fit only to be pruned away and cut off as such from Christ, the Vine, who alone brings forth true life and fruit that will last forever.

Our Union with Christ Is an Act of God

Christ teaches us in his use of the vine and the branches that those who accept his call to be his disciples enter into a living union with Christ. It cannot be the work of our own intellectual pursuits; this union is solely the work of the Holy Trinity of Father, Son, and Holy Spirit. St. Paul explains this in a similar way: "But if Christ is in you, though the body is dead because of sin, the Spirit is life because of righteousness. If the Spirit of him who raised Jesus from the dead dwells in you, he who raised Christ from the dead will give life to your mortal bodies also through his Spirit that dwells in you" (Rom 8:10–11). John writes similarly in his First Epistle: "And by this we know that he abides in us, by the Spirit that he has given us" (1 John 3:24).

A Symbiotic Union

So intimate is this union between the Vine (Christ) and the branches (his justified disciples down through the ages) that we can see each is nothing without the other. This intimate union comes about through a symbiosis. There can be no fruitful branch without the living Vine. Jesus stresses this truth: "Just as the branch cannot bear fruit by itself unless it abides in the vine, neither can you unless you abide in me...apart from me you can do nothing. Whoever does not abide in me is thrown away like a branch and withers; such branches are gathered, thrown into the fire, and burned" (John 15:4–6).

We see also that the vine cannot pour out its living grapes without the branches. Likewise Christ needed Mary to mother him into our human race to begin the salvation of the world. He similarly needed his twelve apostles to preach the good news to all who would wish to live by it.

A Vine Needs Branches

All that we are as branches to extend the glorious, risen Lord and Savior into the world through each historical moment in our time and space belongs to God through the Son and the Holy Spirit from the Source of all creation, the Heavenly Father. Thus, we must realize that we belong totally to God through Christ, our Head. We are his members of his Mystical Body, the Church. There can never be any self-centered glorifying of ourselves independent of the outpouring love of the Trinity.

Abide in Me As I Abide in You

In the Gospels, Jesus frequently invited certain individuals to "come to me...." Some Christians have been baptized into the new life through the indwelling Holy Trinity as mere infants. Others as adults have heard Christ's invitation to become his disciples. Hopefully all those Christians baptized in infancy, as adults, have heard seriously Christ's call to "come to me."

John and Andrew, the first-called disciples of Jesus, asked him, "Master, where do you live?" Jesus invited them: "Come and see" (John 1:39; cf. also Matt 11:28).

The Evangelist John shows us that, however we were inserted into Christ as branches to bear much fruit, Jesus gives us another call to "...abide in me as I abide in you" (John 15:4). The invitation of Jesus implies a permanent presence of himself and ourselves individually in an intimate, personalized union that will never cease growing if we cooperate by "bearing more fruit" (John 15:1–2).

Characteristics of True Love

We already pointed out the characteristics of true love as found within the Holy Trinity as a community of love. We can describe this perfect love on our part as our constant striving to be available to the Divine Trinity dwelling within us individually with perfect availability. Striving to live intimately, we wish to share ourselves totally on all levels of our God-given humanity. "As the Father has loved me, so have I loved you; abide in my love. If you keep my commandments, you will abide in my love, just as I have kept my Father's commandment and abide in his love" (John 15:10–11).

Finally, true love demands always within the Trinity and in our intimate relationship with Christ in us "a going forth," an emptying out of the dark depths of ourselves to embrace the cross of bringing death to our false self-centering by putting on the mind of Christ by an inner revolution (Eph 4:23).

The Incredibly Good News

This is the incredibly good news John presents to us. The Vine exists even without the branches. But the branches cannot be true living branches unless they are receiving life through sap from the Vine. "God's love has been poured into our hearts through the Holy Spirit that has been given to us" (Rom 5:5), and "the Spirit of God dwells" in us (Rom 8:9), in order that in his Spirit we might know that we are really "children of God" (1 John 3:1) made "heirs of God and joint heirs with Christ" of heaven forever (Rom 8:17).

Jesus is the way, the truth, and the life, who leads us into the most intimate presence of the triune God, Father, Son, and Holy Spirit who wish effectively to come and abide within us.

Living Consciously in Christ

We praise God most when we live consciously in Christ in order that with his mind we may glorify the Father in his Spirit of Love. We seek always to please the Father as Jesus did (John 13:31–32). Whatever we pray for, it will be granted when we strive always to glorify the Father (John 15:17).

The work of the risen Jesus is to release his Spirit who divinizes us, "regenerates" us, making us beautiful and "alluring" to Christ, the Bridegroom. It is in the "heart," scriptural language for the innermost core of one's being, that we discover our true self in the oneness we enjoy with Christ. He inebriates us with the beauty of his divine-human person. In our heart he meets us in an I-Thou relationship.

Through his Spirit we understand that, just as the Father loves Jesus, so Jesus loves us (John 15:9). He, God-Man, has died for us. That love for each one of us hurled him into a new resurrectional life, which he now at each moment wishes to share with us.

Entering into Deeper Prayer

We enter into this intimacy alone with Christ. Only individually, in deep prayer, can we realize through the Spirit that Jesus' kenotic or self-emptying love for us on the cross is the image of the same love the Father and the Holy Spirit share with him on our behalf. Jesus the Bridegroom continually addresses us in the beautiful words of the Song of Songs: "Ah, you are beautiful, my beloved, truly lovely" (Song 1:16).

For Me He Dies

Jesus tells his disciples in John 15:13–15:

> No one has greater love than this, to lay down one's life for one's friends. You are my friends if you do what I command you. I do not call you servants any longer, because the servant does not know what the master is doing; but I have called you friends, because I have made known to you everything that I have heard from my Father.

Jesus could have suffered and died for all human beings, but he becomes the suffering Servant of God and the perfect Image of God the Father through the hidden Gift of Love, the Holy Spirit. He is always the Father's Word, serving the Father to reveal his great love for us.

Jesus is always loving us unto death, although he will never need to die on the cross again. He is now present in our lives with the same dynamic, eternal love that he had when he died freely to serve us (John 10:17–18). In prayer, especially in the communion of the Eucharist, we can realize that we are now being loved by our infinitely loving Father through the same perfect love of Jesus and the Holy Spirit.

God-Trinity Dwelling Within Us

As we progress in deeper prayer, we grow more intimately in union with God as Trinity, the core of all reality, and we begin to live in the power of their burning love that surrounds us in all things and permeates the depths of our being. Prayer moves away from a "doing" act; above all, from our speaking to God as to an object. We are entering day by day into a constant state of being in his love.

If Jesus loves us as the Father loves him (John 15:9), how did the human Jesus experience this burning love of the Father for himself? Prayer for Jesus meant to adjust his whole being to the presence of the Father and the Spirit dwelling with his humanity. It was surrendering in his human consciousness to the trinitarian God, Father, Son, and Holy Spirit. For Jesus, to pray was to be receptive to God's personalized love at every moment. He strove to surrender to that love by returning it moment by moment by loving the Father through the Holy Spirit as the Father loves him.

For us human beings contemplation is a growth through the infusion of faith, hope, and love by the Spirit of the Father and Son. As we abide in Christ, we grow in greater awareness that the God-Trinity is always present. We contemplate by listening to and receiving God's communicating love for us, always constant, never changing, yet always freshly being revealed to us in the circumstances of our human situation.

The Fullness of God's Love

God can never increase his love for us, for in Christ Jesus has he not given us the fullness of his love? Can the indwelling Trinity be imperfectly present in us? Does God wait for us to tell him that we love him and then he will come to us with a greater love? Does God's love for us become more ardent and perfect after we have performed for him some good work? No!

Prayer must never be our attempt to change God's mind, so he will love us more. It is essentially our "tuning in" to God's all-pervasive presence as perfect love. It is to find him in all things as the power that creates and sustains all creatures in being for "in him we live and move and have our being" (Acts 17:28).

Out of Love Christ Dies for Us

The ultimate way we have of knowing how God loves us is to experience the love that Jesus has for us. This love is given to us as he dies on the cross freely for love of us. But also through his resurrection and the outpouring of his Holy Spirit, he pours that love of himself and of his Father into our hearts through the Spirit they both give us (Rom 5:5).

The "good news" of the triune God living within us can come to us only through God's revelation, known in holy scripture and in the Church's magisterial teaching through many centuries of Christianity. Through the mysteries of the Incarnation, death, and resurrection of the Word-made-flesh, and his giving to us a constant release of the Spirit of Love, we can believe with certainty that, as we die to sin or self-love, we open ourselves up more and more to the eternal, trinitarian community of love within and around us.

The Transforming Love of the Trinity

As we experience the transforming love of the triune God, we should be experiencing more completely each day our being molded by the interior actions of the Trinity. Our filial abandonment to the interior operations of the Trinity, as in the life of Jesus, tends at once also to urge us to move outward toward the world.

From an anonymous world, we find ourselves interiorly meeting the loving and personalized We-Community of Father, Son, and Holy Spirit. The completion of that inner movement is an outward thrust into the world community to be a servant through whom God can actualize a world community of I, Thou, and We—the Body of Christ, the Church, ever-conscious of being the Bride of Christ.

The degree of God's invasion of us, or rather, of how much we surrender to allow his all-invading presence to transform us, is measured infallibly by the testimony of the fruit of the Holy Spirit produced in us as we relate to others (Gal 5:22). Later we will deal with the purpose of Christ's desire to work in and through us: "You did not choose me but I chose you. And I appointed you to go and bear fruit, fruit that will last....I am giving you these commands so that you may love one another" (John 15:16–17).

CHAPTER EIGHT

I Am Crucified with Christ

The English poet Francis Thompson summarized his entire life in one of his last poems, entitled "An Ode to a Setting Sun," with these two cryptic lines:

Nothing lives, but something dies;
Nothing dies, but something lives.

Paradox of True Life

Jesus preached a doctrine that contained many paradoxes, but the greatest is summarized in this saying: "[W]hoever does not take up the cross and follow me is not worthy of me. Those who find their life will lose it, and those who lose their life for my sake will find it" (Matt 10:38–39).

Just as Jesus preached his doctrine, so he lived it. His carrying of his cross to Calvary, his mounting the cross to preach with his dying gasp the saving doctrine of dying to self, only to bear abundant fruit in the resurrection, is a summary of what every Christian's life should be. In our spiritual life, there must be a constant dying to those elements that prevent full growth, so that God-Trinity may live completely in us. Jesus is affirming that if we wish to live in union with him and his Father and be what God destined us to be, loving children of God, bringing forth the fruits of the Holy

Spirit (Gal 5:22), we must die to any dominating forces that take us away from our union with Christ.

This is also necessary if we are to fulfill the great commandments to love, not only God with our whole heart, mind, and strength, but also our neighbor as we love ourselves (Matt 22:37–40).

I Live Now, Not I, But Christ Lives in Me

St. Paul describes one of the chief characteristics of his spirituality, which he strongly lived throughout his apostolic life and also continually taught his new Christian converts through his letters: "I have been crucified with Christ; it is no longer I who live, but it is Christ who lives in me. And the life I now live in the flesh I live by faith in the Son of God, who loved me and gave himself for me" (Gal 2:20).

Paul's Epistle to the Galatians is filled with disappointment toward the members of the Galatian Church. Through his evangelizing them, these early Christians became filled with an abundance of the gifts of the Holy Spirit. But then they turned away from their continued growth in their experiencing of God's indwelling love in them individually and communally and returned to practicing the Jewish Laws. In his letter he asks them: "Did you receive the Spirit by doing the works of the law or by believing what you heard?...Well then, does God supply you with the Spirit and work miracles among you by your doing the works of the law, or by your believing what you heard?" (Gal 3:2–5).

Crucifixion Means Death

Paul had the inspired genius from the Holy Spirit to preach the glory of Christ's ignominious crucifixion as the life-giving power to conquer the curse of sin from the first

I AM CRUCIFIED WITH CHRIST

Adam's fault. This victory over sin calls us also to abide in Christ by meeting him as the Crucified One, by dying to all works of the flesh, and by putting on Christ as sharers of God-Trinity's divine nature. Paul writes:

> For if we have been united with him in a death like his, we will certainly be united with him in a resurrection like his. We know that our old self was crucified with him so that the body of sin might be destroyed, and we might no longer be enslaved to sin. For whoever has died is freed from sin. But if we have died with Christ, we believe that we will also live with him. We know that Christ, being raised from the dead, will never die again; death no longer has dominion over him. The death he died, he died to sin, once for all; but the life he lives, he lives to God. So you also must consider yourselves dead to sin and alive to God in Christ Jesus. (Rom 6:5–11)

Abiding in the Wounds of Christ

As Jesus has taught us that we are to abide or live in him, so also are we to abide in the wounds of the crucified Christ. "There is the place of union, and life, and growth....It is in death that the Prince of life conquers the power of death. It is in death alone that he can make me a partaker of that victory. Each new experience of the power of that life depends upon our fellowship in the death. The death and the life, the Cross and the Resurrection are inseparable."[1]

So many Christians hang a crucifix of Christ in their homes or even carry or wear a small cross. And yet the majority of these Christians, gazing on the crucifix of Christ, think mainly of how he atoned for our sins by dying on the cross, but so few follow St. Paul's teaching: "I have been crucified with Christ; and it is no longer I who live, but it is Christ who lives in me" (Gal 2:20).

Love Unto the End

When Jesus gathered his disciples together for a last meal, he is described as having great excitement in his heart. He had reached a peak moment in his life. Everything from the cave of Bethlehem, the carpenter's home in Nazareth, the desert temptations, and the previous few years of exhausting travels to preach to and heal the multitudes led to this moment: "Jesus knew that his hour had come to depart from this world and go to the Father. Having loved his own who were in the world, he loved them to the end" (John 13:1).

Bringing Fire to the Earth

Periodically during his public life the flaming love in his heart to accomplish what his Father had sent him to do would flare out in words of ardent longing: "I came to bring fire to the earth, and how I wish it were already kindled! I have a baptism with which to be baptized, and what stress I am under until it is completed!" (Luke 12:49–50).

His baptism would be of water and blood poured out from his loving heart, the heart of the suffering God imaged in Jesus. When the spear opened his heart and there poured forth the last drops of water and blood, then Jesus' work was consummated: "It is finished" (John 19:30).

The Definitive Word of Love

What is accomplished? The purpose of the Incarnation. God in man has now finally spoken his definitive Word of love in Jesus Christ. St. John, the beloved disciple of Christ, invites us to "see" the Word being spoken clearly, the Word telling us at that moment of God's infinite love for all human beings. The horrendous folly of the sufferings of Christ is sheer nonsense except in terms of the logic of Divine Love!

For the contemplative Christian, poor in spirit and pure of heart, the complete self-emptying *(kenosis)* even to the last drop of blood and water has fullest meaning only in being an exact image of the heart of God the Father in his infinite, tender, self-sacrificing love for all of us.

Eternal, Divine Love

We human beings would always have entertained some doubt as to the infinite love of the Father for us unless he, who so loved us as to give us his only begotten Son (John 3:16), was being imaged perfectly in Jesus, poured out unto the last drop of water and blood on the cross. Not even the omnipotent God can speak another word beyond his Word spoken in utter emptying-unto-death in Jesus. Beyond creative and free suffering-unto-death, there is no other language in which both human and divine love can be adequately expressed. "Do not be afraid; I am the first and the last, and the living one. I was dead, and see, I am alive forever and ever; and I have the keys of Death and of Hades" (Rev 1:17–18).

Nonbeing

The Christian life has been described by Jesus Christ and his disciples as a death-unto-life experience. He described this life as a denial of one's self, as a shouldering of one's cross and following him (Matt 10:38, 16:24; Mark 8:34; Luke 9:23, 14:27). Jesus insisted that the seed had to fall into the earth and die before it could bring forth greater fruit (John 12:24).

Law of Inner Growth

Made according to "God's own image and likeness" (Gen 1:26–27), we possess the ability with God's grace to stretch ourselves upward to attain new levels of transcendent meaningfulness by letting go of lower levels of being. Holy scripture presents this conversion process in terms of an *exodus,* a passing-over to a state of becoming progressively free in the darkness and sterility of the desert that leads to the Promised Land.

Psychologists speak of it as a twofold movement. The first stage consists of accepting ourselves with honesty and without excuse. This is a moment of awakening, revealing the truth that what we thought was our actual personhood was in reality a false self. Many of us seek various ways of escaping from this self-knowledge, such as worldly distractions, preoccupation with work or travel, or simply mindless inactivity.

Élan Toward New Life

Only if we learn to accept sincerely our existential self can we ever hope to open up to the second movement: namely, to hunger and thirst in the totality of our being to be someone more noble, more loving, more in our oneness with God-Trinity and neighbors and the entire universe. This is the *élan* toward new life. This is True Being calling us to experience our true selves in the Source as a unique manifestation of God's presence in human form on this earth.

But this only can follow the letting go of the false self and all the protective devices and techniques we have been using to secure the lie that the illusory person is the true self. And how most of us detest the thought of the dying process that will yield to new life! How afraid we are to enter into the depths of our unconscious in order that we might become more conscious of our beautiful, unique self as we bring the brokenness in our heart to the healing power of the indwelling Love itself.

Intermeshed in Humanity

We know from holy scripture and the history of the human race how we form a solidarity with the whole world in our brokenness, in "the sin of the world." We find our darkness to be a part of the world's darkness. We have inherited it simply by being a part of the human race. We share also in the brokenness and "worldliness" through the Body of Christ, the Church. Paul writes: "We know that the whole creation has been groaning in labor pains until now; and not only the creation, but we ourselves, who have the first fruits of the Spirit, groan inwardly while we wait for adoption, the redemption of our bodies" (Rom 8:22–23).

Interdependence on Others

All of us are interdependent on others, not only for our very being, but for being who we are. We inherit in birth, not only the values of our parents, but through them the values of generations and generations that preceded them. What an amazing world of interrelationships microbiology opens up to us.

Each of the one-hundred-trillion cells in your body contains about 100,000 different genes composed of DNA (deoxyribonucleic acid). Each DNA molecule stores coded information to be used to sustain and duplicate itself. Through such dependency upon our parents, we receive, not only similar physical traits, but also much of their positive and negative qualities. We share in their brokenness even before we see the light of day.

The Innermost True Self

Whatever the skein of knotted, twisted threads that have fashioned the tapestry of our lives, there lies deep within us another self, the true self of unrealized potentiality. In our brokenness we are driven into our creaturely nothingness. What can we do to extricate ourselves from the overpowering forces that have mostly come originally from without, but now lie within, like unchained, wild dogs within us?

Deep within us lies our real self, the unique person unrealized as yet, but loved infinitely by the triune God. God's Spirit hovers over this chaos, the darkness that could blaze forth into creative light, peace, and joy if we would only stretch out and follow that thin silvery streak of godly light out of the binding slavery into true freedom. It is here in our true self that God dwells, making his "mansion" within us (John14:23) as we become more and more spirit, communicating freely unto intimate loving communion with Christ and the Holy Spirit as we share in their divine energies of love to become children of the one Heavenly Father.

God's Healing Love

To live on this level of loving union with the indwelling Trinity is to burst the bonds of predeterministic forces within us and to step out of the cave of crippling, stifling darkness into the bright day of spring. Only God is powerful enough to aid us in being "reborn" again by his Holy Spirit of love (John 3:3–5). Only in experiencing the healing love from a tender, loving Father made manifest through the Spirit of the risen Jesus can we rise from the brokenness of our past experiences to embrace a new level of a life in Christ, which is, as God always intended, to become our real self.

No longer do we have to be locked in the prison of our narcissism, to obey our carnal-mindedness or the dictates of others as the sole criterion of truth. Our habitual low profile with all of our defenses or painful inadequacies is replaced by an authentic humility that shows us from God's view our true self in the light of God's special gifts and endowments. Honesty and sincerity become like two bright shining beacons that dissipate any self-deceit from whatever cause.

Free Children of God

This is a call to live in the freedom of being children of God. But it is a frightening call that demands daily courage to encounter the *daimonic* forces of darkness and the new potential for greater aliveness to God's loving presence everywhere. It is within ourselves that we must enter in the honesty and poverty of spirit that is the silence needed to hear God speak his still-pointed Word.

Into the tomb of our inner darkness, the light of God's tender love bursts upon us. Tears of sorrow and repentance, tears of fright at our "nonbeing" pour forth gently as God's soft, healing dew falls upon the cracked, parched earth of our heart to stir those seeds of new life into reality.

Lost But Now Found

As we utter the words, "Have mercy on me, O God, according to your steadfast love" (Ps 51:1), we continually hear his healing response that thrills us into new life: "...this son of mine was dead and is alive again; he was lost and is found" (Luke 15:24).

The death-dealing Cross is where we can meet Christ as our risen Redeemer. As we bear our crosses daily by dying to our own self-centeredness and arrogant pride, we can by God's grace experience the indwelling Trinity as the Father, Son, and Holy Spirit in Christ's *new creation:* "So if anyone is in Christ, there is a new creation: everything old has passed away; see, everything has become new! All this is from God, who reconciled us to himself through Christ, and has given us the ministry of reconciliation" (2 Cor 5:17–19).

CHAPTER NINE

The Eucharist and the Holy Trinity

Have you ever noticed that a difference takes place in your relationships with friends when they invite you to eat a meal at their table? The food and drink are symbol-carriers that make it possible to "act out" a mysterious, spiritual reality that we call love. Not only is human interiority expressed through this action of self-giving, but feelings and movements become a transforming power far beyond what was locked up inside the human heart.

God's Loving Gift to Us

The Eucharist is the place in our human space and time where, in a similar "meal," God reaches, as it were, the peak of his inner trinitarian love. The tremendous mutual self-giving of Father and Son and Spirit of Love cannot contain itself. It wants to burst forth, to be shared with us. God gives himself to us as he in creating us endows us with so many gifts.

But the Eucharist is the center of all presences of God toward us and summarizes all of God's other gifts to us. In the Eucharist, we touch the basis of all reality, the Holy Trinity. Here are concentrated the uncreated, personalized, loving energies of God as a loving community. God's fullness of infinite love moves toward us in order to transform us into being his loving children.

The Importance of the Mystery of the Incarnation

What makes Christianity unique among all other religions is the mystery of the Incarnation. Not only non-Christians, but also many who believe themselves to be true followers of Christ find it difficult to embrace the paradox that God so loves the human race that he became irrevocably a part of humanity when his only begotten Son "became flesh and lived among us" (John 1:14).

Throughout history certain people have opted more for the divinity in the person of Jesus Christ, to the weakening or complete denial that he was truly human. This was at the basis of Docetism and Monophysitism, two heresies that in substance denied that God would have anything to do with matter.[1] Other groups claimed that Jesus was totally human and that God "adopted" him as his divine Son. Such "adoptionists" were called Arians after their leader, Arius, who denied that Christ was the pre-existent Word of God.[2]

Because Christian theologians for many centuries stressed the divinity of Christ, some modern theologians seek now to accentuate his humanity. They gather their ideas about Jesus mainly from the Gospel narratives. In such a view, Jesus is seen as a mere man, born as all of us human beings are born. He grew and developed through life experiences as we do and gradually he came to a realization that he was the Son of God. In such a view, Jesus cannot be considered the pre-existent Son of God.[3]

The Church

As Christians conceive of Jesus Christ, so they develop and live out a doctrine of the Church. If Jesus is conceived of as being more divine than human, the Church becomes a disincarnated body, fleeing from world involvement. If Jesus is seen as more human than divine, the Church develops as a humanistic agency, a "do-gooder" institution that can hardly be discerned as any different from a civil or social organization.

In the early Church, Jesus was not scrutinized and dissected into parts, to the destruction of the whole Person. The Church was a living body of people baptized into the trinitarian life. These Christians met together in a spirit of humble contemplation and adoration to celebrate God's revelation of love in history, especially in the mystery of the Incarnation, death, and resurrection of Jesus Christ, the only begotten Son of God.

Offerers of Christ and of Ourselves to God

As a community in prayer, the early Church not only heard the Word preached, but they also literally received the living Word, God-Man, Jesus Christ, in the Eucharist. They entered into the act of the Eucharist, the liturgy (the prayer of the faithful), to become offerers of Jesus Christ to God and to become those offered in Jesus Christ.[4]

One of the earliest Eucharistic texts, the Didache, formulates the Christian community's prayer: "As this broken bread was scattered upon the hills and was gathered together and made one, so let thy Church be gathered together into thy kingdom from the end of the earth."[5]

The Eucharist: Peak of Trinitarian Love

Our Christian faith finds its climax in the Eucharist. All presences of Jesus in our material world meet in the Eucharist and are transcended and superseded by this unique presence. The Eucharist is the climax of God's self-giving to us and, therefore, contains all other forms of his presence "toward" us. Now we have the means whereby we can enter into the fullness of God's intimate sharing of his very life with us, through touching the glorified, risen humanity of Christ in the Eucharist.

Not only do we receive the entire, historical Jesus of Nazareth, with all his earthly life of teaching, preaching, healing, and performing miracles—the greatest of which is his passion and death on our behalf—but also we receive the risen Lord of glory with the presence of the entire blessed Trinity. Our faith reaches its peak in the Eucharist as we, a praying, adoring community, surrender to the mysterious, transforming action of the Trinity, Father, Son, and Holy Spirit. Here are concentrated the uncreated, loving energies of God. God's fullness of love moves toward us to transform us into his loving children.

The Goal of the Incarnation Is Eucharist

In the Incarnation, "God so loved the world that he gave his only Son" (John 3:16). Out of this mystery of his infinite love for us flows the Eucharist. As the gift of the Eucharist is possible only because of the gift of the God-Man, the Logos-made-flesh in the Incarnation, so the mystery of the Incarnation leads us ultimately to the mystery of the Blessed Trinity.

"Whoever has seen me has seen the Father" (John 14:9). Who receives the Body and Blood of the Son of God receives not only the Son, but also the Father in his Spirit of Love. Who abides in the Son abides in the Father, who comes with the Son and his Spirit to dwell within the recipient of the Eucharist. "Those who love me will keep my word, and my Father will love them, and we will come to them and make our home with them" (John 14:23).

Thus, the three mysteries—the Eucharist, the Incarnation, and the Trinity—intimately connect and explain each other.[6] The mysteries of the Trinity and the Incarnation are rooted in God's essence as Love. As the Trinity seeks to share its very own intimate "family" life with others, the Word leaps forth from the heart of the Father into our earthly existence:

> For while gentle silence enveloped all things, and night in its swift course was now half gone, your all-powerful word leaped from heaven, from the royal throne, into the midst of the land that was doomed, a stern warrior carrying the sharp sword of your authentic command, and stood and filled all things with death and touched heaven while standing on earth. (Wis 18:14–16)

God's Word inserts himself into our material world, taking upon himself the form of a servant (Phil 2:8), like unto us in all things save sin (Heb 4:15). Not only does God wed himself to the entire, material universe by assuming matter into the trinitarian family, but God also touches each human being. Through the Incarnation, through the humanity of Jesus Christ, all human beings are made one. He is the new Adam, the true firstborn of the human race. We are destined to live with him and through him the very life of God's only begotten Son from all eternity.

The Depths of the Trinity's Love for Us

The Eucharist brings this oneness with Christ to fulfillment. Our relationship to the Trinity is not one of an extrinsic adoption, but analogous to the true Sonship of Jesus Christ. In giving us in the Eucharist his very Body and Blood as food and drink, Christ wishes to share his very own life with us (John 6:57–58). The Father has the fullness of life, and he has communicated it to his Son.

Jesus Christ, the image of the Father in human form (Col 1:15), pours his very own life into all of us who wish to partake of his flesh and blood. He is the "Living Bread," the Bread of Life that comes down from heaven. In the Incarnation he took upon himself our human nature. In the Eucharist we become assimilated into his human-divine nature.

It is staggering to our weak minds and impossible to comprehend adequately the depths of God the Father's love for us imaged in his only begotten Son. It is in fact that we become one with God's only Son. We are engrafted into his very being as a branch is inserted into the vine and becomes one total being (John 15:2–6).

Incorporated into Christ

We share in the Eucharist in Christ's own life, that life of the historical person Jesus Christ, now gloriously resurrected. We are personally incorporated into Christ without losing our own identity. Christ lives in us, but we must always be further formed in him: "My little children, for whom I am again in the pain of childbirth until Christ is formed in you, I wish I were present with you now and could change my tone, for I am perplexed about you" (Gal 4:19–20).

In the Eucharist, God opens to us "the unsearchable riches of Christ" (Eph 3:8). He loves us in the oneness of the infinite, uncreated, loving energies of the Trinity. We join our hearts to that of the God-Man and praise and worship the Heavenly Father with a perfect love and in complete self-surrender with the Holy Spirit.

Union with the Blessed Trinity

In our oneness with Jesus Christ in the Eucharist, we are brought into the heart of the Trinity. Here is the climax of God's eternal plan and the essence of eternal heaven, when "he chose us in Christ before the foundation of the world to be holy and blameless before him in love" (Eph 1:4). Along with an intensification of our own I-Thou relationship with Jesus, the Holy Spirit brings us into a new awareness of our being also one with the Father and his Holy Spirit. This is the essence of the Last Supper Discourse of Jesus as recorded in John's Gospel:

> I ask not only on behalf of these, but also on behalf of those who will believe in me through their word, that they may all be one. As you, Father, are in me and I am in you, may they also be in us, so that the world may believe that you have sent me. The glory that you have given me I have given them, so that they may be one, as we are one, I in them and you in me, that they may become completely one, so that the world may know that you have sent me and have loved them even as you have loved me. (John 17:20–23)

The Fruit of the Eucharist

The glory that the Father gave to Jesus was to raise, through the Incarnation, his human nature into a oneness with his "natural" state of being the only begotten Son of the Father from all eternity. That same glory in the Eucharist Jesus is sharing with us to be, by the power of the Holy Spirit, one with his Sonship. We are raised to a supernatural relationship with the Blessed Trinity. We become by the fruit of the Eucharist, as the Byzantine liturgy of St. John

Chrysostom puts it, through the fellowship of the Holy Spirit, "true participants of the divine nature" (2 Pet 1:4).

Receiving Also the Trinity

If we receive, as we truly believe, the total Jesus, true God and true man, we also receive the Father and his Spirit. For the Son cannot be separated from the glorious union he enjoys with the Father. This is more than a moral union. The Son has received everything that he is from the Father. Unlike an earthly father or mother who begets a child and the act of its creation is finished, the Heavenly Father is continuously pouring the fullness of his being into his Son.

Jesus clearly said, "I am in the Father and the Father is in me" (John 14:10). More clearly yet, Jesus said, "[T]he one who sent me is with me, he has not left me alone" (John 8:29).

A Temple of the Holy Spirit

If Jesus and the Father abide in each other and have come to abide within us in the Eucharist (John 12:23), the Holy Spirit, as the bond of unity that brings them together and who proceeds as love from their abiding union, also comes and dwells in us. How fittingly applicable are the words of St. Paul to our reception of the Eucharist: "[D]o you not know that your body is a temple of the Holy Spirit within you, which you have from God, and that you are not your own?" (1 Cor 6:19).

Again Paul describes the indwelling Spirit as accompanying the love of God in our hearts: "God's love has been poured into our hearts through the Holy Spirit that has been given to us" (Rom 5:5). In the Eucharist, we experience par excellence the Father begetting us in his one Son through his Spirit. "You are my son; today I have begotten you" (Ps 2:7).

In a way, we can say the Father loves only one person and that is his own Son, Jesus Christ. But he loves us with an infinite love as he loves us in him. What reverence ought to be ours as we open our hearts to the perfect love of Jesus for his Father! What joy should flood us as we experience the infinite love of the Father being generated freshly for us in each reception of the Eucharist as he loves us in Jesus!

Union with Each Other

In the Eucharist we are not only united with the Trinity, but we also attain a new oneness with the others in whom the same trinitarian life exists, especially within the context of the eucharistic celebration. Here is where the Church, the Mystical Body of Christ, comes together in loving union with its Head, Jesus Christ. The liturgy, or the "work" of the people of God, has to be always the context (except in emergencies such as communion given to the sick and dying) in which the Eucharist is received. The liturgy is the sacred place and time when the Church is most realized by the power of the Holy Spirit. It is the vehicle by which we praise and glorify God for the gifts of life and salvation we have received.

In the Eucharist Christ's Members Are United

It is especially in the reception of the Eucharist that all members of Christ's Body are most powerfully united in a new sense of oneness with each other. They symbolically enter into the depths of the richness of God's self-sacrificing love. The Eucharist is not only a sacrament, but it is also the ever-now sacrifice of Christ for us to the Father unto our healing and redemption. It is the culmination of all the sacraments as encounters with Christ in his self-giving to us, for in the Eucharist Jesus Christ gives himself as he did in the first eucharistic celebration of the Last Supper before his death and on our behalf, but with Jesus and the Father abiding in us and their Spirit of Love empowering us to do that which would be impossible for us alone to do consistently.

We are born spiritually as God's children, brothers and sisters to each other as we truly live the sacrament of baptism that reaches its fullness of loving union between us and God and between one another in the Eucharist. This is the central scope of the Eucharist, the union of all the faithful through the mutual union of each individual with the Holy Trinity. The Eucharist creates the unity of all who participate in the same Bread of Life.

Transformation by the Holy Spirit

Therefore, we not only receive Jesus Christ in the Eucharist in order to praise God the Father and surrender ourselves to him in the same self-surrendering act of Jesus Christ on the cross, but we are also to be transformed interiorly by Christ's Spirit: "Be renewed in the spirit of your minds" (Eph 4:23). By praising and glorifying the Heavenly Father, we open ourselves in the Eucharist and at all times after the Eucharist to his transforming blessing that he breathes upon us to make us a true, effective, eucharistic blessing to all whom we meet.

We put on the mind of Christ in the Eucharist when we face with him a broken, suffering world. We become a living part of the Body of Christ, we become Church, when we share the caring love of Jesus for each suffering person we meet. Pain gnaws at our hearts as we suffer the pain of the heart of Christ not to be able to do more for the poor and afflicted in all parts of the world. We suffer in our own inadequacies that do not allow us to know what we can effectively do to alleviate the physical and moral evils rampant in the world.

The Trinity Is Present in All of Creation

With St. Paul we can ask whether we have truly received Christ's Body in the Eucharist, if, after the liturgical celebration, we do not receive as a brother or sister of our one Father each human being who enters into our lives (1 Cor 11:27–29).

As we become more conscious of the indwelling Trinity brought to such a peak of experience in the Eucharist, we join the gifts of creativity placed within us by God's graces with the working power of the triune God—Father, Son, and Holy Spirit. We live each moment in the resurrectional hope that is engendered in the social and historical horizontal.

Instead of running away from involvement in the activities of this world, we Christians should move to the "inside" presence of the Trinity at the heart of matter. What anyone of us adds to make this world better in Christ Jesus has an eternal effect on the whole process. When the love experienced in the Eucharist becomes the dominant force in our lives, then every thought, word, and deed is bathed in the light of the indwelling Trinity inside the whole world.

Called to Be Eucharistic Ministers

We are called to live in this reality of the pervasive, loving presence of the Trinity acting through the mediation of the God-Man, Jesus Christ. This is the true Christian contemplative. As we celebrate the divine liturgy, our faith makes us vividly aware of this trinitarian presence, when, in microcosmic fashion, Jesus the High Priest breathes over a small segment of the Church, including the gifts of bread and wine, and his Spirit of Love transfigures that part of the incomplete world into a sharing in Christ's divine nature.

The authentic Christian contemplative extends this transfiguring liturgy throughout her or his day in every thought, word, and deed for God's glory. No matter how insignificant, banal, and monotonous our work may be, we are to be vibrantly aware of Jesus Christ, already glorified, living within us and working through us to bring the whole world to its fullness.

All Is Now Sacred

As communion with the Body and Blood of Jesus brings the contemplative Christian into the dynamic presence of the Trinity, so this communion with him is extended into the materiality of each day. The false division between the profane and the sacred ceases as we prayerfully contemplate the Holy Trinity in all of creation.

Contemplation flows from the fullness of our activities because we find the Trinity in the very activity of the moment. We discover divine richness in the most commonplace action. We find the Holy Trinity at work for the redemption of the human race and we become an instrument to that end.

New Eyes to See the Holy Trinity Everywhere

We have new "eyes" with which to see, not only the uncreated energies of the one God essentially working out of love, but also to see and experience the Divine Father become our Father and the Father of all our brothers and sisters. We see the Son, not only always adoring the Father in total self-surrendering love, but we also see him as our Head, while we are parts as members of his total, complete Body.

We experience the loving presence of the Holy Spirit, not only binding the Father and Son into a oneness that calls out their uniqueness of persons, but also binding us, all other human beings, and the entire material universe into a oneness of the Body of Christ with a uniqueness assigned to each individual human person and each material creature.

For such modern contemplatives, there should be no "insignificant" event that does not bear the stamp of the Holy Trinity's actively involved, loving presence touching the world through the humanity of Jesus, now joined to that of the person of prayer in order to bring it to completion according to the original plan as conceived by the Holy Trinity. Such a contemplative patiently lives day by day in the mystery of the Trinity's presence in one's life and shuns any objectivizing of this awesome mystery of God both as one and as three loving relationships to each other and to ourselves.

The Trinity Is Actively Involved in the World

To the little ones of this earth, the poor of spirit and clean of heart, God reveals through his Holy Spirit how simple bread and wine can open them up to the Bread of Life, Jesus Christ, true God and true man. They see the world as a part of the eternal liturgy that the Lamb of God is offering to the Heavenly Father, with the presence of the risen Jesus abiding therein.

The heart of all reality is Eucharist: receiving God's great love for us in his Son incarnate, through the illumination of the Holy Spirit, who empowers us to return that love in self-surrendering service to each person we meet. It is in Eucharist that we submit ourselves in humble adoration of the Holy Trinity.

Chapter Ten

May Your Joy Be Full

At your funeral, would your friends remember you as a very joyful person? Be honest with yourself. Are you always joyful? St. Paul writes to the early Christian converts of Philippi: "Rejoice in the Lord always; again I will say, Rejoice!" (Phil 4:4). So if you are a Christian what prevents you from being always joyful?

Perhaps in our present time we are plagued, more than any other previous generation, with the problem of the meaning of our human existence. We are faced with mounting invisible powers of evil in our society, the world over, along with our own burden of guilt for the disharmony within ourselves and around us. Death threatens any meaningful existence and destroys any possibility for genuine joy.[1] Yet the gift of joy is not anything we can develop through positive thinking. It is one of the great gifts from the Holy Spirit (Gal 5:22–23). Deep down in all human beings God has implanted the burning desire to be loving, joyful, and radiant in an everlasting happiness that nothing can ever take away from us. Such a joyful love demands also that we are available in joyful readiness to live for the happiness of all whom we meet. To be so available we must look upon all others with a joyful hope in their innate goodness. It is a call to a mutuality of an I-Thou relationship.

Yet this necessitates our readiness to die to selfishness and to embrace the suffering out of which joy can emerge and flow out as gift to others.

As Gold Is Purified by Fire

As joy is the gift of the Holy Spirit, we cannot receive the gift unless we are purified of all the impediments within us. This is the work of the Holy Spirit. What determines whether we are willing to meet God-Trinity in greater faith, hope, and love and in continued joy is how willing we are to surrender to the purifications and pruning that God effects in our lives (John 15:1–3).

It is, therefore, inwardly that we are to go to find God as the Source of our being. It is there that we will discover our true freedom as a joyful child of a loving Father. Beyond all preconditionings of our false selves, our past training, our thought patterns, even our sins, we enter deeper and deeper, down into the depths that push to claim new areas of conquest in the dark recesses of the unconscious.

There is so much more of you to come into being if you only would have the courage to enter into the interior battle and allow God to purify you in the depths of your being! God is calling you constantly into a process of letting go of the controlled activity you have been exercising in your prayer life and in your attempts to imitate the virtues of Christ Jesus through your own power.

Absolute Surrender

As you let go of your own self-centeredness, you will move into deeper levels of abandonment that are rooted in your dissatisfaction of yourself, in your sinful darkness that you now find lying below the surface of your habitual consciousness.

Along with this increased dissatisfaction with your own illusory activities to heal yourself of your disharmony toward God, faith, hope, and love, and your abandonment to God's loving presence, also increase to a new pitch that far exceeds the sense of God's presence earlier experienced in affective prayer.

Totally surrendered to God, you live now only for him as each moment brings you an occasion to be a loving gift back to God. A new threshold of union with God has been reached as God takes away from you all your attachment to sense pleasures. Nothing or no one can now be the source of any attraction without a conscious submission of that relationship to God's holy will.[2]

I strongly believe that the necessary condition for obtaining God's full blessing and our awareness of the indwelling in us of the Blessed Trinity, which only makes possible that our joy may be full, comes from our absolute surrender in continued free will to do the will of the Trinity in each event of our daily life.

Dancing in Synchronicity with the Trinity

In the poem "Little Gidding," T. S. Eliot pointed out the condition we must pay to recover our lost paradise:

A condition of complete simplicity
(Costing not less than everything)

At some time or other, perhaps when we least expected it, you and I have experienced the presence of God come upon us in such an overwhelming intimacy of his love. Such moments are joyous openings to the transcendent beauty of God. It seemed that we broke through our "earthly" time as a measurement of length and space and entered into God's eternal presence as uncontrollable life and beauty.

I will share with you the most joyful day I ever experienced in my life. I shall never forget the sense of simplicity of God-Trinity dwelling with me, around me, present in all creatures. My joyous oneness that filled me with a unity of God as the core of my being is still vividly present to me even all these years later.

A Spiritual Happening of Twenty-four Hours

This joyful at-oneness with me happened in January 1974, when I was already a Jesuit for thirty years. This "happening" lasted a full twenty-four hours, all through one day and the night, until the morning of the following day. There was no sleep. I was so alive to God's inner life, so full of his triune abundant love. Why should I sleep when I was cradled in the cosmic arms of my Heavenly Father? I was consciously aware of my being permeated in every part—body, soul, and spirit—with the Trinity's personalized, uncreated energies of love!

Functional time disappeared, as I felt immersed in God's eternal timeliness. There was perfect synchronicity between the transcendent Trinity—Father, Son, and Spirit—and myself. I was dancing with God and all the creatures of his cosmos in perfect rhythm. I was a child again, laughing with tears of joy that I never wanted to end. Yet there were also tears of sorrow, bittersweet. How blind I was not to have lived before in this joyous, natural rhythm, one with God and all of nature with this same awareness!

Dead to God's Harmony

How sad that millions of human beings are dead to God's harmonious rhythm, that they live lives so deprived of this joyful, childlike abandonment to the divine source of all life! What could I do, I thought, to bring other human beings into this inner simplicity of God-Trinity, calling all of his children to share the triune multiplicity in oneness?

It was too awesome an experience to yield to any desire on my part to encapsulate it in order to call it forth at will against the boring and frightening aspects of future, meaningless situations. And yet I have never forgotten that experience in all its vividness. But more importantly, the truth that sounds so clearly with me at all times since then is this: The opposite of true joy, the gift from the Holy Spirit, is not sorrow, but "disbelief."

Christ's Promises to Give Us His Joy

I believe that it would not be an exaggeration to say that all human beings, made in the image and likeness of Christ, are continually searching for what we think will bring us joy. Can we not believe that the essence of heaven will be a continued growth of the joy we have developed by cooperating with the Holy Spirit during our lifetime on earth to live in his gifts of love and joy?[3]

Jesus gives us in the gospel teachings several basic texts that give us his will and that of the Father through the working of the Holy Spirit that we might share in the infinite joy of the Blessed Trinity. The Trinity has revealed through Christ's teachings that the gift of joy is a vital part of God's plan of salvation on our behalf.

We must first be convinced that Jesus has promised, while he was still on this earth as God-Man, to share with us his very own joy. He told his twelve disciples in the three Last Supper Discourses: "I have said these things to you so that my joy may be in you, and that your joy may be complete" (John 15:11).

Chosen by God-Trinity

Jesus began this section making it very clear that it is he and the Heavenly Father who have chosen us and anointed us by their Holy Spirit out of their mutual love and joy. Jesus promises to give us a share that is of his very own joy. His joy comes to him in his early life as he strove always to be obedient in his human will to please his Heavenly Father. Yet he could not at the Last Supper share that joy until he reached the ecstatic joy on the cross as he surrendered himself in his great statement: "It is finished." Such Christ-joy could only be given to us after his death, resurrection, and ascension into glory.

The author of the Letter to the Hebrews well understood Jesus' perfect love and joy: "[T]herefore God, your God, has anointed you with the oil of gladness beyond your companions" (Heb 1:9; cf. Jas 5:14). Jesus spoke a second time about his sharing with his disciples his joy that would be given to them in fullness only after his resurrection: "So you have pain now; but I will see you again, and your hearts will rejoice, and no one will take your joy from you" (John 16:22).

Your Sorrow Will Turn to Joy

Jesus continues to prepare his disciples that their sorrow will come when he will die the next day on the cross, and that they will also suffer in the future for preaching Christ to the world, even unto great persecutions. This reference that his disciples' sorrows would turn to joy can always include his faithful disciples down through all earthly time. We must remember, when we find sufferings and great sorrows in our following Jesus, that he will always give us a share of his perfect joy to overcome all sorrows.

Jesus gives us a guarantee that no one will ever be able to take this joy away from us. He uses the example of the mother, who, in giving birth, undergoes great physical and psychic sufferings. "When a woman is in labor, she has pain, because her hour has come. But when her child is born, she no longer remembers the anguish because of the joy of having brought a human being into the world" (John 16:21).

Now faithful disciples also can bear all sufferings, even death itself, because of this new relationship made possible through his promise given in his farewell discourses to his apostles before he freely died out of perfect love for each of us followers. It is because of who Jesus is and what he did that our joy can overcome all sufferings in him who strengthens us in our "thorn of the flesh" (2 Cor 12:9–10).

Jesus Promises to Share His Joy with Us

Jesus promises his disciples a third time that he will always share his joy with them. This is found in his priestly prayer addressed to his Heavenly Father in John's Chapter 17. Jesus prays so tenderly and powerfully to his Father that his chosen disciples will be one always, as he is one with his Father. As High Priest, Jesus asks his Father a request, which he never ceases to offer on behalf of all his disciples in his Church even now and forever: "Holy Father, protect them in your name that you have given me, so that they may be one as we are one….But now I am coming to you, and speak these things in the world so that they may have my joy made complete in themselves" (John 17:11–13).

In Jesus We Place All Our Trust

In light of the promises Christ made to us and his first disciples that his joy will abide in us always, St. Paul teaches us the importance of our trust and hope in Christ as the Way, the Truth, and the Life (John 14:6):

> I pray that the God of our Lord Jesus Christ, the Father of glory, may give you a spirit of wisdom and revelation as you come to know him, so that, with the eyes of your heart enlightened, you may know what is the hope to which he has called you, what are the riches of his glorious inheritance among the saints. (Eph 1:17–18)

The first part of surrendering love is that we accept God-Trinity wholly and entirely. We let God take complete possession of our lives. We cannot reach out to God, not even to accept his love and joy, unless the Holy Spirit inspires us to that belief, hope, and love. The Spirit's primary grace is to inspire us to "want" God.

God Loves Us Because He Wills to Do So

But his gift inspiring me to want to possess God follows upon the most primary graces: that God, prior to anything else in our regard, has always loved us. With utter freedom flowing from his holiness, and with absolute perfectness, God loves us simply because he wills it. God is love, and love pours itself out as a kenosis, an emptying, and a pouring-out toward us. Our faith through the power of the Holy Spirit confirms us of God's eternal love for us. This is the basis for our Christian hope in and through Christ to the heart of the Heavenly Father.

The Weakness of Our Hope

Hope recognizes humbly our own weakness and utter inability to love God or to be loving in his regard. But hope places all our strength in God's goodness and holiness. When we fathom something of the "unfathomableness" of God and let ourselves be abandoned to this love, that is hope. In faith I accept God for his love. In hope I accept God for his "unfathomableness," which will remain in varying degrees for all eternity.

But the greatest difficulty to exercise faith and hope in and through Jesus lies within us. Jesus promised, as we saw in the texts above, that no one would ever take this joy from us. Yet in substance he often pointed out that we must be vigilant against the world, the flesh, and the devil. As Paul experienced in his own life: "Sin dwells in my members" (Rom 7:24).

The Valley of Our Nothingness

Jesus preached that we must enter into our heart and cleanse it from within (Matt 23:27). The early church Fathers and Mothers who were moved by the Holy Spirit to go out into the fiercest deserts in Egypt discovered that the closer they approached the awesome indwelling of the Holy Spirit within them, the more they shed tears for their sinfulness. As they looked upon the inner mountain of God's grandeur, the more clearly they saw the valley of their own nothingness. They experienced in the tomb of their inner darkness the light of God's tender love bursting upon them, and ever so softly and healingly tears welled up in their eyes. With King David they prayed constantly: "Hide your face from my sins, and blot out all my iniquities. Create in me a clean heart, O God, and put a new and right spirit within me" (Ps 51:9–10).

Whoever Abides in Christ Does Not Sin

John writes in his First Epistle: "You know that he was revealed to take away sins, and in him there is no sin....Those who have been born of God do not sin, because God's seed abides in them; they cannot sin, because they have been born of God" (1 John 3:5–6, 9). These statements might surprise many Christians, who may not realize the distinctions that John and also Paul make between sin in our members, whose roots will be within our fleshly selves, and the state of not sinning.

In his Letter to the Romans, Paul speaks for himself but also for all human beings who have ever lived and will live:

> For we know that the law is spiritual; but I am of the flesh, sold into slavery under sin. I do not understand my own actions. For I do not do what I want, but I do the very thing I hate. Now if I do what I do not want, I agree that the law is good. But in fact it is no longer I that do it, but sin that dwells within me. For I know that nothing good dwells within me, that is, in my flesh. I can will what is right, but I cannot do it. For I do not do the good I want, but the evil I do not want is what I do. (Rom 7:14–20)

Sold as a Slave to Sin

John equivalently writes as Paul does in describing our sinful nature: "If we say that we have no sin, we deceive ourselves, and the truth is not in us. If we confess our sins, he who is faithful and just will forgive us our sins and cleanse us from all unrighteousness" (1 John 1:8–9).

Have Mercy on Me, a Sinner

Then immediately John adds about our past sins: "If we say that we have not sinned, we make him a liar, and his word is not in us" (1 John 1:10). We might ask ourselves this: If we have sin in our bodily members, how can we escape from committing actual sins?

The answer is found over and over in the earlier chapters as the reason for the Incarnation, Christ's teachings, and his promises to abide within us as he shares with us his very own divine nature and if we in turn abide in him and accept his indwelling power over all sin. In Jesus, "we do not have a high priest who is unable to sympathize with our weaknesses, but we have one who in every respect has been tested as we are, yet without sin. Let us therefore approach the throne of grace with boldness, so that we may receive mercy and find grace to help in time of need" (Heb 4:15–16).

Abide in Me As I Abide in You

St. Francis de Sales was fond of saying that there never has been a "sad" saint! If we abide in Christ as he, the risen Lord, God-Man, abides in us and releases within us the fruit of the Holy Spirit of love and joy, how could we ever not

> rejoice in the Lord always; again I will say, Rejoice. Let your gentleness be known to everyone. The Lord is near. Do not worry about anything, but in everything by prayer and supplication with thanksgiving let your requests be made known to God. And the

peace of God, which surpasses all understanding, will guard your hearts and your minds in Christ Jesus. (Phil 4:4–7)

We Christians, who have understood through the Spirit of Love the infinite love of Jesus for each of us, will live more and more consciously in the intimate union with Christ as our guiding force. "Beloved, we are God's children now; what we will be has not yet been revealed. What we do know is this: when he is revealed, we will be like him, for we will see him as he is" (1 John 3:2).

A Divine Friend Dwells within You

If Jesus, so full of love for you, truly abides within you, how can you ever again be sad and lonely? How can you ever be focused solely on yourself and not completely on him, the burning center of love living within you and in the entire universe?

Is it difficult for you now to keep in contact with him in his infinite, ever-now love for you unto death? No matter how weak you are, when you are aware of such a friend living within you, giving you courage to become one with him in all that you do and think and say, you can accomplish infinitely more than what you could do alone, "for apart from me you can do nothing" (John 15:5). Peace and joy of the Spirit govern all thoughts, words, and deeds because you have experienced in him the infinite love and omnipotence of God. This love is not far away, but abides within your very heart, your deepest consciousness through the gifts of the Spirit of faith, hope, and love. No force outside can harm you, because "you are from God, and have conquered them; for the one who is in you is greater than the one who is in the world" (1 John 4:4).

Chapter Eleven

How to Live in the Indwelling Trinity

The Hindu poet Tagore, in the decade before World War II, voiced a problem that is still very much contemporary:

> Civilization is almost exclusively masculine, a civilization of power in which woman has been thrust aside in the shade. Therefore, it has lost its balance and is moving by hopping from war to war. Its motive forces are the forces of destruction and its ceremonials are carried through by an appalling number of human sacrifices. This one-sided civilization is crashing along a series of catastrophes at a tremendous speed because of its one-sidedness. And at last the time has arrived when woman must step in and impart her life rhythm to the reckless movement of power.[1]

Animus vs. Anima

Modern psychology describes the integrated human person as a harmonious blending of two psychic principles. The *animus* is the intelligible principle of analysis, which gives birth to critical reflection, to control and calculation. The *anima* is defined as the principle of relationships, of communion and unity.[2]

Woman and man make contact with God in a "feminine" relationship, an attitude of reverence and waiting for God to take the initiative to reveal himself. If he is always present and, therefore, always revealing himself to us, and if we are not always seeing him and listening to him in his revealed Word, "shining diaphanously" (to use Teilhard de Chardin's favorite expression) through the material world, then it is because we have not developed the contemplative side of our human nature.

I use the term *inscape,* coined by Gerard Manley Hopkins, to suggest this contemplative attitude of Christians going inside of matter to find there the uncreated energies of the immanent Trinity, loving and serving us unto our healing and happiness. For Hopkins, inscape is the "outward reflection of the inner nature of a thing." He defined it in 1886 as "the individually-distinctive beauty" of each creature.[3]

It is this "thisness" or "selfing" that makes every inanimate or animate creature a distinctive individual. For St. Maximus the Confessor, it is God's gift to the pure of heart to see his Logos in each creature and adore that Holy Presence by working with God's Mind to reconcile all things to God.

An Exhausted Spirituality

In our exploding universe of today, the traditional views presented by Western Christianity and based largely on an exhausted scholastic philosophy and theology, concerning human beings, God, and the material world, no longer seem adequate. A spiritual vision is needed to offset the Augustinian Platonism that has accounted for an unchristian separation of nature and supernature and a heavy dichotomizing between our human body and soul, matter and spirit, the secular and the sacred.

Our heavy rationalistic framework that has served to present Christianity to the West is in need of a complementary vision. Such a "new" vision is really not so new. It is found in the Old and New Testaments and is grounded more in perceptual, intuitive knowledge. It is an openness to mystery in which we can meet the transcendent God in a reverential awe and wonderment. Yet God's transcendence cannot separate him from us. We are rooted in God as in our Ground of Being.

The Transcendent and Immanent God

Yet that Ground, because God is so completely transcendent, is also rooted immanently within us. As Jesus Christ is the meeting of divinity and humanity with neither of them inseparable, and yet each of them distinct, so also we, in all of our materiality and finite humanness, are not to be separated from God living within us, even though God is not a human person and we human persons will never become God.

The uncreated energies of God touch all of us. Our created energies touch God. The divine and human co-penetrate each other. They are inseparable from each other, yet each other possesses its unique "otherness" and distinction.

God is calling all of us to become contemplatives, not in spite of the world, not by running away from an evolving, material world that at times perhaps groans in travail louder than it whispers songs of glory to God, but precisely by running into the world. There God is everywhere. It is for us, with pure hearts that have been emptied of all selfishness, to open our inner eyes to see him there. We adore him in awesome worship. We also adore him as we give ourselves to build the earth into the Body of Christ. Only the Christian contemplative will survive in the future, both as a Christian and an authentic human being, for only such a person will be growing daily in love of God and loving service of neighbor. The rest of human beings will be "dead souls," ravaged by the specter of meaninglessness in their lives.

Faith, But Not Living It Out

All the preachers who have preached to us throughout our Christian life readily give intellectual assent to the statement that God is a Trinity, a community of three distinct Divine Persons, Father, Son, and Holy Spirit. But let us be honest and ask: Why is it that most of our preachers rarely if at all ever preach about the indwelling in us, if we are in the state of sanctifying grace of the Blessed Trinity? I believe that they find it very difficult to preach this most important revelation, which Jesus revealed to us through his disciples.

It is incredible that such a dogmatic truth upon which Christianity depends should be believed in by our intellectual assent but never do we think of living out such a revealed truth in our daily living, a truth which we find in so many New Testament texts, especially in the Johannine and Pauline writings.

Reality Is God Dwelling within Us

The French Cardinal Mercier, in a retreat he preached to priests a few months before the First World War, said:

> Reality is God dwelling within us. Many baptized souls are ignorant of this mystery and remain their whole lives unaware of it....The very people whose mission is to preach it throughout the world neglect

it, forget it, and when it is brought home to them are astonished.[4]

The Indwelling Doctrine of God in Us: Myth, Metaphor, or Reality?

I believe that most Christians know that the New Testament writings and the teachings of the Church, from Christ's first disciples down to the magisterium, have taught us to accept this dogma. They may even vaguely believe that God dwells within their hearts; that with St. Paul, they believe their very bodies are temples of Jesus and the Holy Spirit abides within us.

But how few Christians daily live in the mystery of the indwelling Trinity in them and allow this doctrine to have great and practical applications as they allow Christ to live his resurrected life in them throughout the day and night!

St. Ignatius, Martyr

In the first three centuries of Christianity, this doctrine of the indwelling Trinity was the solace of the early Christians who went to their martyrdom in their belief that heaven was already their abode, as the indwelling Trinity accepted their burning love. I would like to highlight the writings of St. Ignatius, who was Archbishop of Antioch and martyred in Rome (c. 35–c. 107).

Ignatius was ordered from Syria to Rome to suffer martyrdom for his Christian faith. On his way to Rome, he wrote letters to the Christians of Ephesus, Magnesia, Tralles, and Rome. From Troas, he wrote letters to the Churches of Philadelphia and Smyrna and to Polycarp of Smyrna. His simplicity of style, his scriptural language, his idioms, and above all his emotional and passionate devotion to Jesus

Christ along with his ardent faith and passionate desire to die for Christ, true God and true man, made his writings very popular among early Christians of the first three centuries.

Influenced by St. John and St. Paul

The foundation of Ignatius's teachings on Christology and ecclesiology is solidly influenced by the writings of St. John and St. Paul. His mysticism is based on Paul's idea of union with Christ, joined to John's idea of life in Christ, and there we see the high ideal of Ignatius's teachings: to put on the mind of Christ by allowing Christ to live his virtues in the intimate union with fervent Christians. Ignatius addresses himself as *Theophoros:* the God bearer. Christians are called by him to be *Christophoroi:* bearers of Christ.

We see this from this following citation of his letter to the Ephesians: "You, therefore, as well as all your fellow-travelers, are God-Bearers, Temple-Bearers, Christ-Bearers *(Christophoroi),* Bearers of Holiness, adorned in all respects with the commandments of Jesus...because with respect to your Christian life you love nothing, but God only."[5]

In the preceding chapters of this book, I have tried to lay the spiritual and dogmatic foundation that now, in this chapter, I offer by way of a summation of our main theme on the indwelling of the Holy Trinity.

Living Out the Revealed Truth of Christ's Indwelling Presence

I would like to quote from an anonymous Latin monk's description, which would be typical of so many writers from the thirteenth century to our present time. Then we can focus on how we can live out in our daily lives this foundational truth that Jesus Christ revealed to us through his disciples, from whom we have received it in the New Testament writings and in the traditions passed down as clarifications through the working of the Holy Spirit in the Church magisterium.

This unknown thirteenth-century monk writes about the mystery of the resurrection whereby Jesus Christ inhabits us from within:

> In me, in my most interior Jesus is present. All outside of our heart is only to discover the treasure hidden interiorly in the heart. There is found that sepulcher of Easter and there the new life. "Woman, why do you weep? Whom do you seek? Whom you seek, you already possess and you do not know him? You have the true, eternal joy and still you weep? It is more intimate to your being and still you seek it outside! You are there, outside, weeping near the tomb. Your heart is my tomb. And I am not there dead, but I repose there, living always. Your soul is my garden. You are right when you believed that I was the gardener. I am the New Adam. I work and supervise my paradise. Your tears, your love, your desire, all this is my work. You possess me at the most intimate level of your being, without knowing it and this is why you seek me outside. It is then outside also that I appeared to you and also that I make you to return to yourself, to make you find at the intimacy of your being him whom you seek outside."[6]

Christ Dwelling within Us

Your growth in spiritual perfection consists of the intensity of the union that we attain through the conscious awareness we have of Jesus Christ living and operating within us as we surrender ourselves totally to his inner guidance. We strive to live in a perfect symbiosis, a life with him of two wills operating in love as one, through the union brought about by the Holy Spirit.

This living Christ is given to you in the fullness of his resurrectional life. Yet in a way, this intimate, loving union of yourself with Christ can be compared in the beginning to an embryo that is to grow illimitably, both now on this earth and forever in the relationship we call heaven. We are to cooperate with Christ by yielding to his indwelling presence as we move away from our own petty self-centeredness and surrender to his guiding light.

Paul as a Midwife

St. Paul considered his role as a midwife to bring forth the life of Christ into the hearts of his Christian converts. And this life, he considered, developed as the individual Christian surrendered to the lordship of Christ risen.

> For the weapons of our warfare are not merely human, but they have divine power to destroy strongholds. We destroy arguments and every proud obstacle raised up against the knowledge of God, and we take every thought captive to obey Christ. We are ready to punish every disobedience when your obedience is complete. (2 Cor 10:4–6)

Jesus Lives in Us by the Power of the Holy Spirit

It is only through the Holy Spirit released by the indwelling, risen Jesus that we can know the full Jesus Christ and our true selves in loving oneness with him. "And by this we know that he abides in us, by the Spirit that he has given us" (1 John 3:24). This Spirit of Love fills us with faith in

God's great love in Christ Jesus and faith in that living and loving Christ abiding intimately within us. We are filled with hope by the Holy Spirit that the risen Lord has conquered sin and death, and we can meet this indwelling, risen Lord in all of our darkness and inauthenticity.

The Spirit fills us with the hopeful realization that our fully integrated persons, the ones that we should be by God's unique love for each of us, can be realized only by the interacting, loving relationships of the Father, Son, and Holy Spirit.

Abide in Me As I Abide in You

We Christians, who have understood through the Spirit of Love the infinite love of Jesus for each of us, will live more and more consciously in this intimate union with Christ as our guide. "Think of the love that the Father has lavished on us" (1 John 3:2). If Jesus, so full of love for you, truly abides within you, how can you ever be lonely? How can we be focused solely on ourselves and not completely on him, the burning center of love living within us and in the entire universe?

Is it difficult for you now to keep in contact with him in his infinite, ever-now love for you unto death? No matter how weak you are, when you are aware of such a friend living within you, giving you courage to become one with him in all that you do and think and say, you can accomplish infinitely more than what you could do alone. "For apart from me you can do nothing" (John 15:5).

The Entire Trinity Dwells within Us

In Chapter 9, we showed how we receive in the Eucharist, not only the full Jesus Christ, the glorious risen God-Man, but also the Heavenly Father and the Holy Spirit. Now we affirm that the presence of the three Divine Persons is not limited, as in the Eucharist, to the consecrated species. If we are in the state of sanctifying grace, the Trinity dwelt in our soul before our receiving the Eucharist and they remain after the species disappear. But the triune presence is more intimate since the Eucharist has increased in our souls the greater intimacy of the Trinity indwelling within us. "…[A]nd my Father will love them, and we will come to them and make our home with them" (John 14:23).

The Personalized Love of the Trinity

Abiding within our souls, the Trinity of Father, Son, and Holy Spirit act unceasingly since they share within their triune community the one divine nature that is *love*. And yet we are loved differently by each Divine Person. As M. V. Bernadot, OP, writes: "This love is single, because each time that the three Persons act exteriorly to themselves, they act as one. At the same time it is a triple effusion of love, revealing something of the characteristics proper to each of the three Persons."[7]

Each Person of the Trinity Is Unique

The Father is present as the Source of all life. The Word is the communicative who speaks as the only Word of the Father, and through the Holy Spirit we can not only hear God's Word of love and power but we will also be empowered by ever-deepening faith, hope, and love of the Spirit to respond to the Word. The Holy Spirit is the mutual love proceeding from the Father to the Son and vice versa. The Spirit unites himself to my free will to bring me into the supernatural love of the Father and the Son.

Perhaps we can now understand more clearly what Blessed Elizabeth of the Trinity meant when she wrote: "I have found Heaven on earth, because Heaven is God and God lives in my heart."[8]

How Does the Triune God Dwell in Us?

We will never be able to answer this with rational concepts since we are brought back again to the awesome mystery of the inner life of God's essence or divine nature. No mere human person could ever "see" God and know the Persons of the Trinity as they are, in their one and the same divine nature (John 1:18; Exod 33:20). We would have to be God to know with God's very own divine nature.

According to certain writers, who rely on trustworthy historical tradition, handed down in particular by the early Greek Fathers, and especially by St. Cyril of Alexandria (d. 444), it is by the Holy Spirit that the Father and the Son abide within us. There are, as it were, two stages, not in chronological, but in logical order, which is called formal causality.

The Mystery of the Circumincession

The Holy Spirit, by baptism, takes possession of our souls. This is the first stage. Because of the circumincession *(perichoresis* in Greek)—by which the Holy Spirit, the Gift of love from Father to Son and vice versa, is found—the Father and Son are likewise present. Immediately after the coming of the Holy Spirit, the Father and the Son become equally present. This is the first point and the second is this: In what manner, precisely, is produced within us the union of God with us, and of us with him? In the early decades of the twentieth century, Scholastic theologians, especially the

Dominicans and Jesuits, formulated their causal answer, based on the writings of St. Thomas Aquinas, especially on Aristotle's four causes.[9]

A Knowledge Beyond All Understanding

Now theologians since Vatican II have given up the Scholastic method of explaining how the Blessed Trinity abides within the faithful living in sanctifying grace and have returned to a knowledge that surpasses understanding so that

> Christ may dwell in your hearts through faith, as you are being rooted and grounded in love. I pray that you may have the power to comprehend, with all the saints, what is the breadth and length and height and depth, and to know the love of Christ that surpasses knowledge, so that you may be filled with all the fullness of God. (Eph 3:17–19)

This is a great mystery, which is at the center of the reality of the indwelling Trinity within us. We cannot understand the mystery of transubstantiation with our own human understanding, yet our faith is more certain than any intellectual explanation of how Christ is present in the eucharistic species of bread and wine. So also we believe through the gift of the Holy Spirit that Jesus and the Father dwell within us (1 John 3:23), though we cannot know in an exhaustive way, by our own rational minds, the inner life of the Trinity and how it indwells us through God's sanctifying grace that flows from the incarnate Word of God who reveals such mysteries: "Long ago God spoke to our ancestors in many and various ways by the prophets, but in these last days he has spoken to us by a Son, whom he appointed heir of all things, through whom he also created the worlds" (Heb 1:1–2).

What Can We Do to Live in the Holy Trinity?

Cardinal Newman has defined the true Christian as a person absorbed by a feeling of the presence of God within him or her; a person living in this thought that God is there, in the depths of his or her heart; a person whose conscience is illuminated by God to such an extent that he or she lives in the habitual impression that each of his troubles and every fiber of his moral life, his every motive and desire, are spread before the Almighty.[10] Surely this is the way St. Paul lived and taught his converts to Christianity in the first century:

> For through the law I died to the law, so that I might live to God. I have been crucified with Christ; and it is no longer I who live, but it is Christ who lives in me. And the life I now live in the flesh I live by faith in the Son of God, who loved me and gave himself for me. I do not nullify the grace of God; for if justification comes through the law, then Christ died for nothing. (Gal 2:19–21)

We Need to Cooperate with God's Will

The first thing we are to do is to desire "to abide" in the Trinity as the three Persons already abide in us through our living in the state of sanctifying grace. Many Christians believe that the desire to live more and more consciously aware of the indwelling Trinity is a special call from God meant only for certain persons who live in a religious order or belong to the priesthood. We can be absolutely certain that the Community of Love, the Blessed Trinity, has an everlasting will for all of us to live in the indwelling Trinity within us.

We read in the Epistle to the Hebrews: "Jesus Christ is yesterday, today and always the same" (Heb 13:8; KJV). To desire to answer God's call to abide in the indwelling Trinity demands that we are solidly grounded in holy scripture, especially in the New Testament, and seek out writers who are experts in the scriptures and in the teaching of the magisterium, from Christ's early disciples and their successors down through the ages to our present time.

Be Still and Know I Am Your God

Cardinal Newman offers this prayer:

Lord, I am asking for yourself, for nothing short of you, O my God, who have given yourself wholly to us. Enter into my heart substantially and personally, and fill me with fervor by filling my heart with you. You alone can fill the souls of human beings. You have promised to do so. You are the living Flame, and you ever burn with love of all human beings. Enter into me and set me on fire after your pattern and likeness.[11]

And Blessed Elizabeth of the Trinity realistically describes how all who seek to live in union with the Trinity must above all live no longer for themselves:

To love is to forget oneself,
To lose oneself in the Beloved,
Within the burning furnace of his Love.
The true lover lives no longer in himself
But feels the need of ceaseless self-oblivion.[12]

Resting in God's Word

God calls us to receive his love through the communication of his Word in his Spirit of love. But the language of love is silence. If we are to listen to God's Word, we are in need of silencing the noisiness within our hearts and around us in the multiplied world that is orientated in its brokenness toward "sin and death," symbols of self-centeredness and a movement away from God-centeredness.

This state of docile listening to the indwelling Trinity is comparable to the seventh day of rest that the Lord took after his labors of creating the world. It is the new day of rest, the day of *kairos* time, of salvation in which we human beings freely will to do that which most pleases the Heavenly Father according to his Word. "We must do everything we can to reach this place of rest, or some of you might copy this example of disobedience and be lost" (Heb 4:11). This is the positive preparation to which we are called—to cooperate with the indwelling Holy Spirit.

Our Cooperation through Asceticism

The negative elements necessary to return trinitarian love by our active abandonment to please God are the elimination of any obstacles of self-pride and self-indulgence that destroy our inner spirit of recollection on the indwelling Trinity. Our memory, understanding, and will must be constantly under strict discipline. This is what Jesus demands of us when he told his disciples to cleanse the vessel from within.

To enter into the inner reality of God's indwelling presence within you, you need to leave the noise, competition, and all-absorbing anxieties and fears that militate against the silence and calm necessary for you to listen to God as he communicates himself to you. This requires a certain amount of physical silence and tranquility as well as a psychic silencing of your emotions, imagination, memory, intellect, and will.

Why Are There So Few True Contemplatives?

St. John of the Cross writes in *The Living Flame of Love* why so many good persons wish to grow more deeply in the spiritual life and yet fall by the wayside:

> There are many who desire to advance and persistently beseech God to bring them to this state of perfection. Yet when God wills to conduct them through the initial trials and mortifications, as is necessary, they are unwilling to suffer them, and they shun them, flee from the narrow road of life, and seek the broad road of their own consolation, which is that of their own perdition.[13]

There are two kinds of true life: one is beatific, consisting of the vision of God to be attained after our natural death (2 Cor 5:1). The other kind is the perfect spiritual life, the possession of God through the union of love. "This is acquired through complete mortification of all the vices and appetites and of one's own nature. Until this is achieved, one cannot reach the perfection of the spiritual life of union with God (Rom 8)."[14]

We Can Do Nothing Without Christ

Jesus invites us to abide always in him, for cut off from him, the "Giver of life more abundantly," we can do nothing. But united with Christ and therefore with the Trinity, we can do all things and bear patiently, and even with some rejoicing, all sufferings, since Christ is our perfect strength (2 Cor 12:9–10).

Brother Lawrence, who lived in the Carmelite Order in Southern France in the seventeenth century, expresses the importance of allowing Christ to be our inner power through the simple but fervent practice of the presence of Christ with the Father and Holy Spirit: "Let us seek Christ often through this virtue. He is within us, let us not seek him elsewhere. Are we not uncivil, and even blameworthy, to leave him alone, occupying ourselves with a thousand trifles which displease and maybe offend him?"[15]

Luminous Darkness

This highest union, the infused union of the Trinity, in which God communicates himself as Father, Son, and Spirit, can never be achieved by our own conceptual knowledge, but through an immediate, experiential knowledge wherein God opens himself to you. It is not so much that God does something "new and different" to you after years of your own preparation and cooperation through continued purification of your heart from all self-centeredness. The Trinity is always present, the same loving Father, Son, and Spirit, loving you with an infinite, uncreated love.

But when you have cracked open the doors of your heart, you stand before what was always there. "Behold, I stand at the door and I knock. He who opens, I will enter and sup with him" (Rev 3:20).

In a state of humility you break yourself of your own illusory power to possess your life by trying to control both God and others. Then it is that you enter into the reality that always was there.

Climbing the Mountain

With Moses we have to climb up the mountain to reach God by a knowing that is an unknowing, a darkness that is truly luminous. As you separate yourself from all limitations you place on God and from all attachments to your own self-love, you reach the top of the mountain. There in the darkness of the storming clouds, you hear the notes of the trumpet, and you see those lights that no human effort could ever give you. No human mind, no guru, no technique could ever bring you God's personalized gift of himself. God wishes to communicate himself directly to his own adopted children. No one but God can make us participants in his divine nature (2 Pet 1:4). This union with the indwelling Trinity is sheer gift, but the Gift is God himself.

You can change your life gradually by pushing yourself gently under the movement of the Spirit of Love to align yourself in all your being with the being of God as self-giving love. You wish to do all to please God. You no longer live for your own self. Your absolute surrender of yourself to God takes place in the context of your every moment, in the deeds, words, and thoughts that you permeate with your self-giving love to God.

Doing All Things for God's Greater Glory

You have only one desire: but to glorify God. He becomes your magnificent obsession. Every thought, word, and deed becomes motivated by the desire to love God with your whole heart. By striving to become what you are in God's love, you reach the state of inner harmony that is manifested by peace and joy. Only then can you become love toward others, a presence of self-giving to all whom you meet. The true test of how intimately we live in the presence of the indwelling Trinity is how intensely we strive to live intimately with each person who comes into our lives.

Living in the Light of Christ

Is it possible for you, me, and all other human beings immersed in the material world of so much motion, activity, and multiplicity, which requires concentration on the work at hand, to be also centered upon the indwelling presence of the Trinity? Can a teacher, a preacher, a farmer, a housewife, a student, a taxi-driver, an accountant, or an athlete live on two levels at the same time? Can you personally be "yourself" completely on the "outside" level of your ordinary living, in contact with material beings outside of you, and still maintain an "inward" attentiveness to the Divine Guest who dwells within you?

Praying Unceasingly

Paul challenged the Thessalonians, ordinary converts to Christianity from all walks of life, to "pray without ceasing, giving thanks in all circumstances; for this is the will of God in Christ Jesus for you" (1 Thess 5:17–18). To pray always was considered a state of awareness that could be reached by the working of the Holy Spirit in the depths of the heart of the individual as he or she stood vigilant and called out for that presence of God to be realized through the medium of human consciousness.

Moving Toward Center

The secret of living the true Christian life under the guidance of the Inner Light of Christ indwelling at center lies in a continuously renewed immediacy of Christ's presence and his loving activity. If you wish to be consciously aware of

Christ's indwelling presence as light and yield to his guidance, you are called to a continued turning inward to become centered upon your Center.

The Amish have a proverb that we can also apply to our inner attention of loving cooperation with the indwelling Christ: "When you pray to God, do not forget to take up your hoe!" How can we say we love Christ and believe in his indwelling in us and neglect to turn inwardly to renew our faith, hope, and love consciously, and from our humility and sincerity express our surrendering love to Christ? This means the mental discipline of moving our will by our own desire to love God with our whole heart, our whole soul, and our whole mind, for no one, not even God, can do this desiring for us. Our consciousness is the medium by which we come into the already present light of Christ. Jesus teaches us: "For where your treasure is, there your heart will be also" (Luke 12:34).

Remembering the Indwelling Christ

A beautiful, modern Christian, Dr. Frank C. Laubach (d. 1970), offers us much inspiration and knowledge of how we can remember the presence of God often throughout the days and nights of our practical business. Dr. Laubach spent many years as a Congregationalist missionary on the island of Mindanao in the southern Philippines helping a fierce tribe, the Maranaws, a Muslim people famous for their anti-Christian attitudes. He was a linguist specialist and scripture scholar who worked for several years to create for the Maranaws a written language in which they could read about the good news of Jesus Christ, since they had no scriptural language to read or write in any language.

Alone, before his wife and child from Pennsylvania joined him, he wrote about his own attempts to remain more and more consciously present to the indwelling Christ, after having read the writings of Brother Lawrence, the Carmelite Lay Brother.

Striving always to live in the presence of God, Laubach wrote:

> Can we have contact with God all the time? All the time awake, fall asleep in his arms and awaken in his presence? Can we attain that?
>
> Can we do his will all the time? Can we think his thoughts all the time? We do not think of one thing. We always think of the relationship of at least two things and more often of three or more things simultaneously. So my problem is this: Can I bring God back in my mind-flow every few seconds so that God shall always be in my mind as an afterimage, shall always be one of the elements in every concept and precept? I choose to make the rest of my life an experiment in answering this question.[16]

Are You Called to Such a Practice?

Is such a practice possible for you? Only if you are called in a conversion to want to become more present to God intimately present to you, and you are willing to move away from dispersion of your attention to become habitually centered on God. The light of Christ is there within you. Like a leaven, he permeates from within every part of your body and mind and spirit. Each moment is given to you so that you may surrender yourself to his inner light and be transformed also into a sharing even now of his glorious resurrection.

His light within you is not a physical light that you should strive to see. It is an inner, transcendent light that has no form. Yet it is something that can be experienced as "localized" in your "heart," in the deepest levels of your consciousness as a new knowledge and presence that you can, by God's grace and your cooperation, habitually be aware of in ever-increasing degrees. This continued state of living in the light of Christ and surrendering to his lordship is the gift of contemplation.

Jesus Wishes to Live His Virtues in Us

The Church's constant teaching of the indwelling Holy Trinity within us through the sanctifying grace of the Holy Spirit and our incorporation into Christ can be viewed from many points of view. If we are guided by the teachings of the Church, whichever aspect we choose for this purpose will usually lead us to a variety of spiritual approaches with some differences in emphasis or details, and yet there will be always something in common with each other.

Avoid Any Self-Centering

After some forty years of teaching, preaching, and writing books on Christian spirituality and prayer, I have come to the conclusion that most Christians focus, in their spiritual relationships with God and neighbor, primarily on themselves and their own needs, as they see God as an object to whom they address what they determine to be what they think they need. They talk to God and present their needs for bodily, psychical, and spiritual gifts. But they usually are more centered upon themselves as the primary focus and not upon God.

A Heteronomous Spirituality

Most Christians can be divided into three groups. In the first group we seek to obey the externals given to us through the teachings of the Church and to perform certain limited works to gain God's favor by what we choose to do. Some theologians have called this a heteronomous spirituality. This is typified by a religious attitude that places authority outside of the interiorized, spiritual powers of the individual guided by the Holy Spirit. Their view of God is of a God who punishes for the least violation of some extrinsic tradition or law. They become justified by their fulfilling external acts that become the source of salvation.

An Autonomous Spirituality

The second group specializes in autonomous spirituality. This is a reaction against the former heteronomous approach. Paul Tillich defines this group as those who "attempt to create the forms of personal and social life without any reference to something ultimate and unconditional, following only the demands of theoretical and practical rationality."[17]

A Theonomous Spirituality

A third group specializes in theonomous spirituality. This is the more adult approach in which we place ourselves under the interior presence of the Holy Spirit. Such a religious approach is able to inform the heteronomous and autonomous forms with true meaning since it is rooted in the ultimacy of God himself, directly and immediately. It is the fulfillment of the image and likeness of God within us. It is an ongoing process of the "inbreaking" of God into our history that is fashioned by our praxis of disciplining ourselves away from any self-centeredness, which tends to make us fall back into an exclusively heteronomous or autonomous way of operating.

The Mysticism of St. Paul

Today when we use the word *mystical,* we usually imply extraordinary charismatic gifts and special religious experiences. These experiences imply a large measure of subjectivity and by their nature are exceptional. Yet for Paul, the doctrine of the incorporation of the Christian in Christ and transfiguration into him through his grace and our cooperation were nothing esoteric, no delicacy reserved for a few.

For Paul, all Christians turning away from their sinful past in a true *metanoia* (a conversion of one's whole being to God) enter into a permanent union of life in and with Christ. We become matured Christians only as long as we consciously live in this union with Christ. We may or may not experience feelings and awareness of this union with Christ, but these are not essential to the reality.

Neither the mere example of Christ, derived from the Gospels, nor his ideas operate on us in some vague, impersonal way. The very historical person of Jesus Christ, who indwells in the baptized Christian as a spiritual, yet personal, power—this is the Christian dynamic. To be baptized in Christ is to be possessed by his person. Paul was "apprehended" by Christ (Phil 3:12), so that the principle of his thought, words, and deeds was no longer Paul, the natural man, subjected to the laws of the flesh, but Christ, "who lives in me" (Gal 2:20).

Putting on a New Life

Paul seized on the reality of this relationship to Christ and never tired of seeking different metaphors to bring out its vivid truth. He speaks of the life of Christ within the Christian as a new life that must be put on, not by some few, but by all Christians. The perfect love of Jesus, the God-Man, did not end with the grave. Many of us Christians may give an intellectual assent to the truth that the risen Lord Jesus really does live within us. To live no longer ourselves, but to enter into the mystical union of living in the glorified, risen Christ—"yesterday, today and always the same" (Heb 13:8; KJV)—is to allow Jesus to become "localized" in our historical "now" moment of time and place.

As long as we Christians focus upon our developing "our" virtues, helped by God's indwelling presence of granting the grace to imitate the virtues Jesus developed all his thirty-three years on this earth, we will be focused on ourselves and miss completely Paul's mystical vision. This perfect consummation of Christ's passionate love, freely dying on the cross, was to thrill his Heavenly Father through the Holy Spirit and to "seize" us to share his union as children of God and brothers and sisters of Jesus.

Absolute Surrender

Jesus, as it were, is repeating from within us what Proverbs 23:26 tells us as in prophecy: "Son, give me your heart." Paul believed that he no longer lived according to his own will, but through the indwelling of Christ risen, Christ lived within him with the perfect love to continue as he did on the cross and when he rose from the dead. This is Paul's constant wish: to glorify the Father, now in Christ through the union of his faithful members with the risen Lord. As

Jesus in the Last Supper prayed so powerfully to his Heavenly Father for his apostles, so he prays continually on the behalf of today's Christians

> "...that they may all be one. As you, Father, are in me and I am in you, may they also be in us, so that the world may believe that you have sent me. The glory that you have given me I have given them, so that they may be one, as we are one, I in them and you in me, that they may become completely one, so that the world may know that you have sent me and have loved them even as you have loved me. (John 17:21–23)

Building Up of the Body of Christ: The Church

From a Christology of individual sanctification, we are led by the mystical vision of Christ to an ecclesial Christology. Absorbed with this new life in Christ, Paul moved easily between the levels where he found this new life in a process of dynamic, progressive growth, namely, the level of the individual, and that of the Christian community. He gives small attention to distinguishing whose perfection is being built up, the individual Christian's or that of the total Christian community, the Church.

The reason is that he saw these levels, not as distinct areas of activity and life, but as two points of view of the identical reality, the life of the risen Christ, living in both the individual and in the united members of his Body, the Church. Furthermore, Paul knew that no individual's sanctity could grow outside of the organism that he fondly called the Body of Christ. The Church grew in sanctity as the life of Christ developed in the individual being.

Summary of Our Intimate Union with Christ

Throughout the preceding chapters, we have seen an array of phrases to describe the one and same union between us Christians and Christ. This union means always the living and loving relationship from the side of Christ risen who abides in us in the fullness of his love. From our side of the relationship, we live in Christ and we can grow progressively in greater unity with Christ as we cooperate with God's grace.

Because this union, brought about by the divinizing power of the Holy Spirit, is a living intimacy between Christ and ourselves, it admits of an ever-increasing growth in faith, hope, and love. "You were taught to put away your former way of life, your old self, corrupt and deluded by its lusts, and to be renewed in the spirit of your minds, and to clothe yourselves with the new self, created according to the likeness of God in true righteousness and holiness" (Eph 4:22–24).

Paul tells the Philippians what he does and what all Christians should do also in this growing union with Christ. He considers all other things a loss or "so much rubbish" in comparison with his desire to gain Christ (Phil 3:8–9). He knows he lives in Christ, but he also realizes that there is still "sin" in his members (Rom 7:20–23). And for this reason he continues his pursuit in hope, "not that I have already obtained this or have already reached the goal; but I press on to make it my own, because Christ Jesus has made me his own" (Phil 3:12).

A Renewal of Our Mind and Spirit

Paul sees our union with the indwelling Christ as a real, objective state as he always experienced in his lifetime on earth the total, risen Jesus Christ. However, this union of a Christian and Christ does not mean for Paul (as it must not mean for us) that it is ever a substantial union that would result in one person, who would remain Jesus Christ, through an absorption of our unique existence.

Alfred Wikenhauser cites B. Bartmann, insisting that through our union with Christ, the new creation of 2 Corinthians 5:17 "makes a physical change in our spirit and its capacities, and the new life which we receive is something real. But this physical change is not substantial. It is merely accidental, and so it does not produce an indelible natural effect. Its effect is in the order of grace, and it may be undone."[18]

Union with Christ Is Never a Static Relationship

This intimate union between ourselves and Christ is a mutual presence, a compenetration, a reciprocal unity, and a mutual sharing of each other in self-sacrificing love (Gal 3:28–29).

Paul's mystical union between Christ and ourselves can never be a static relationship. He never sees the individual reaching a point of perfect union with Christ that will cease from "stretching" forth (*epekteinomenos* in Greek: one who "strains forward as a runner in a stadium"). Paul writes: "I do not consider that I have made it my own; but this one thing I do: forgetting what lies behind and straining forward to what lies ahead, I press on toward the goal for the prize of the heavenly call of God in Christ Jesus" (Phil 3:13–14).

The Process of Deification

Paul never holds out as the fruit and goal of our union with Christ any ecstatic feeling of losing one's selfhood to be forever transformed into divinity. In the process of being divinized through the Spirit of the risen Christ, we are alive to Christ and called to be his ambassadors (2 Cor 5:17–18).

By cooperating with the Spirit's infused faith, hope, and love, we are called to bring the transforming power of Christ's new life into our very time and space. Having experienced the healing love of the risen Jesus, living within us and abiding there with his eternal Father through his Spirit of Love, we are empowered to take our broken moment in the history of the human race, to take our place in this disjointed history, in order to transform them into a new age.

Finally, Paul gives us the authentic measure of how intimately we live in Christ and allow him and his Spirit to work in our lives. That test of our union with Christ through the transformation of ourselves into living members of the Body of Christ is seen in our loving care and service to other beings who come into our lives. To return the love of God that abounds in our hearts through the power of the Spirit (Rom 5:5) must mean for all Christians a burning zeal to bring forth God's creative, healing power that makes us "reconcilers" (2 Cor 5:18) of the entire world to God.

A Burning Zeal to Share Christ with Others

Paul's mystical vision is never a form of Quietism,[19] without any thrust outward to build up the Body of Christ. It is a continued, active response to return love for loved experienced as we live in the "new creation " in Christ (2 Cor 5:17). As we die to our own ego-centered, false self, we will see in our oneness with Christ that we are already risen in the Body of Christ.

The entire world will look different to us. No longer will we see it solely in the light of the Fall, but in the light of Christ risen, for the world is God's, not the devil's! The resurrection of Jesus becomes the force that spirals the whole universe back into the arms of God from whom it was first born. What happened to Jesus in the resurrection is already happening to us as we rise with him and it will happen to the human family and to all creation in the end times.

Christ: The Alpha and the Omega

Christ is the Alpha and the Omega (Rev 1:17). He is at once the center of the material world and its destination, recapitulating the entire cosmos back to the Father, "…and through him to reconcile all things for him, making peace by the blood of the cross through him, whether those on earth or those in heaven" (Col 1:20). As we must be changed by many deaths to our false egos and birthed into our true identity, made "according to the image and likeness" (Gen 1:26) that is Jesus Christ, so must the dark corruption of our ego-mangled world dissolve into light.

God's Gardeners

We do not merely return to our primitive state of Eden at play in the fields of the Lord, but we become the gardeners, unlocking every clod, every lump of matter, that it might grow, bear fruit, nourish the fullness of the "new creation" in Christ. Finally, at the consummate Omega of the material world, wrenched into glory by the birthing hands of God, there will be, as St. Paul saw, the union of Christ with all of God's material creation coming into its fullness and maturity in Christ so that "Christ is all and in all" (Col 3:11).

Transcending Action

People at different levels of personality development and prayer life express the inner core of being where their outflowing energy approximates closely the divine act of creation.

We displace all selfishness and open ourselves to Christ within us, not to imitate his virtues, but that we offer him ourselves so he can relive his earthly surrender to glorify the Father in and through our individual thoughts, words, and actions. For Jesus by his life and the redemption of mankind made for himself a mystical body, in which he continues to live, to love, and to glorify his Father. In order to love the more, he has united himself to new individual human natures, to millions of individual human natures, not hypostatically, it is true, but still by a very real, intimate, and wonderful union.

Paul De Jaegher expresses this mysticism of Jesus' love for his Father and all human persons made by God according to the image and likeness that is Jesus Christ, God-Man.

The Total Christ

The complete Christ is the Christ united to the concourse of the faithful, who will live for ever; the complete love of Christ is the love of the heart of Jesus, united to the love of millions of Christians, who will love with him and in him to the end of time. This is the great masterpiece the Divine Lord has accomplished. This alone has succeeded in quenching the infinite love-thirst, which Christ has for his Father.[20]

The more a person, on a purely secular level with no reflective reference to God, gives up his or her selfish aggrandizement by thinking of and helping others, the more she or he prepares for a fuller living according to the human nature God destined for all of us. The more you can do, by exercising your faith in God's loving and working presence in your life and through your activities to fashion the Body of Christ, by striving with greater purity of heart and fidelity to God's uncreated energies of love, the more alive you will become. You will live out of God's love, for love of God, in God's love. You will surrender yourself to God's infinite power within you and within the moment, and experience freeing in every action you perform in awareness of your intimate union with Christ, his Father, and the Holy Spirit.

Do All for the Greater Glory of God

You learn to experience that everything becomes physically and literally lovable in God. You discover how God can be possessed and loved by you in everything around you. You no longer make an act of love while you are working. You now habitually love while you are working. You are becoming love in every thought, word, and deed. "Whether you eat or drink, or whatever you do, do everything for the glory of God" (1 Cor 10:31).

Every breath you breathe is an act of love. You literally are praying all the time (1 Thess 5:17), for you are seeking always to give God more glory and honor through your intimate union with Christ. He is becoming your God as you "excentrate" out of your self-centeredness, and move yourself into the burning bush of God's triune presence within you and within each creature that you encounter.

Christ Is Being Formed in Us

His cosmic heart is becoming one with our human heart in a very real, ontological way as we yield ourselves more perfectly to his direction. Charged with the living presence of Christ, one in union with the Heavenly Father and the Holy Spirit, we are christified human beings, living within an ever-expanding universe, called to extend the process of christification to hasten the day when the lines of the evolving universe and the evolving Christ in his members will converge in the Omega Point.

Then we will understand Paul's summation of the universe and God's eternal plan in Christ Jesus: "For in him all the fullness of God was pleased to dwell, and through him God was pleased to reconcile to himself all things, whether on earth or in heaven, by making peace through the blood of his cross" (Col 1:19–20).

Conclusion

Science can offer to us a world of great potentiality, surging ever forward in a dynamic movement to greater complexity in unity. It can present to us an objective world of reflected beauty and quasi-order that allows us by faith to come to know much that is objective about the infinite and inexhaustible power and perfect love we call God-Trinity.

To those human beings who walk with humility of heart and integration before God-Trinity (Mic 6:8), the heart of Christ is discovered as an open, pierced heart of Jesus on the cross. It is through this emptied heart on the cross that the small group of "little people," God's *anawim,* can find an entrance into the depths of God's very being as emptied love for each of us, his adopted children.

In that pierced heart of Jesus we can also discover the perfect love of God for all of his creation in and through his Logos-made-flesh and his Spirit. We can touch the cosmic heart[21] of Christ, but only as we live in the depths of our true being, our hearts, in a unity-in-difference with the heart of Christ. Heart calls to heart. How deeply your heart has entered into the heart of Christ and how much of God's fire of love you have allowed to touch yourself are measured by how much fiery love you show in service to others.

We Are Called to Be God's Cooperators

We are called by God-Trinity to be cooperators to explicitly draw out the core of inner fire of God's love at the heart of all matter. The more we can act with full consciousness and reflection, the more we humanize ourselves and the more we unleash the spiritual powers that enable us to transcend the material, the limited, and the particular, and to pass over to the realm of enduring and limitless spirit.

We are privileged by God's call to manifest his heart of healing love to the broken and downhearted. This can come about by living in our heart within the heart of Christ. We bring his flaming heart into this cosmos by unveiling the cosmic heart of Christ in our oneness with him to make it possible that he might unfold, like a nurturing mother, the universe God has created as a mirror reflecting a perfect, humble, all-powerful love. This love is experienced as a pierced heart, poured out, that we human beings may also be a heart pierced by divine love to be love for each other and all of God's cosmos as we assist in the birthing of the universe into the total, cosmic Christ, and help to reconcile the universe to the Father through his Son in his Spirit.

Steps Toward Recollection

Here are some suggestions to help you become centered upon the indwelling Trinity, living within you:

- Seek early in the morning to become centered upon the indwelling Trinity. And before going to bed, re-center yourself in their presence.
- Throughout the busy day, find moments in which you can re-center yourself in God's holy presence with an act of love and surrender.

- Seek to pull yourself together physically, psychically, and spiritually. See that there are no excessive, immoderate actions, thoughts, or words brought forth on any level that would not be unto God's glory.
- Begin obeying God in this present moment with the love that you possess for God. Love begets love, and obedience out of love is the way love is engendered.
- When you find yourself turning away God-Trinity, your Center, humbly acknowledge your diffusion and scatteredness and beg God's strength that you may try again in love to be more faithful to God.
- Be rooted in God's strength as you seek always to work with him and for his glory. Especially in difficulties, learn to surrender yourself to his power in that moment.

Whatever means you take to remain in the loving presence of God as you strive to be more recollected and centered upon him can serve only to make God supreme in your life, and thus you daily seek to love him with your whole heart. You will see great progress in prayer and perfection as you eradicate, with God's power, the roots of selfishness.

As God becomes more and more your Center, you will enjoy greater peace and joy, which no one can ever take from you.

Chapter Twelve

Heaven Bound

We have in these preceding chapters dealt primarily about God-Trinity—Father, Son, and Holy Spirit—in their loving, sanctifying graces given to us as we cooperate.

By deeply exercising faith, hope, and love in the abiding presence of the Blessed Trinity, we saw how we were to live in joy and humility as we put on the mind of Jesus Christ by glorifying the Father, Son, and Holy Spirit. This work would be incomplete if we did not develop what comes when we enter into the eternal inheritance that our Lord has been asking his Father to give us (John 17:21–26).

There has always been in the hearts of human beings a desire to ponder what the future of our lives and of the entire present world will be. Today, more than ever, with advanced technology available, we moderns are becoming even more concerned about the future. "Futurology" is the science that seeks to understand the future and to provide tools whereby we can obtain greater control over our destiny. The surface of planet Earth is exploding with developing sciences and technologies, but the efforts to harness these skills, to develop the earth's resources, and to share them with other inhabitants in peace and love, have met largely with uncoordinated helter-skelter results.

The Theology of Eschatology

The difference between sheer science about the future of planet Earth and what the Church, through divine revelation, has taught us in its knowledge about the future of the world, is the difference between simple growth toward fruition and the need of something new to enter into the process. Jesus Christ risen is that something new, that lifegiving leaven, that has entered into the potentiality of the universe. This is what is called in theology, *eschatology*.

Eschatology is the section of theology that deals with questions concerning the end of our lives and of the entire world. The word is derived from the Greek word eschaton, which means the "end," or the last things. It usually concerns such questions as death, judgment, heaven, hell, purgatory, the resurrection of the dead, and the *Parousia,* or the second coming of Christ.

The Second Coming of Christ

Christ is risen and is in glory before the throne of his heavenly Father. The saints and angels also share in his eternal glory. Yet other members within the Body of Christ still live in the "not yet."

From the original followers' experience of Jesus' first "unveiling" of his glory in the resurrection appearances recorded in the New Testament, the Church has always longingly looked forward to a full "unveiling." *Parousia* is the Greek word that the Church uses to describe that second coming of Christ in glory at the end of time.

Our Christian faith has maintained, down through history, consistently and strongly, the teaching that Christ will come at the end of time to transform this universe by bringing it to its completion in and through himself.

The Final End of God's Creation

"When all things are subjected to him, then the Son himself will also be subjected to the one who put all things in subjection under him, so that God may be all in all" (1 Cor 15:28).

Jesus is already present in this material universe with his risen glory and power, bringing about victory over the dark powers of cosmic evil. But in a true sense, his victory will be perfect only at the end of time and this is the usual sense in which we use the term *Parousia,* or Christ's second and final coming. Christ will appear in all his glory when his Body, the Church, with all its members, angels, and saintly human beings, who will be the "contact" instruments of Christ risen to the material world, will manifest more perfectly than now, in this "not yet condition," the fullness of Christ, the total Christ, the Head, and his members. This will mean that the Gospel will have been preached and lived throughout the entire universe.

A Harmony Among All God's Creatures

This is a most important teaching that is quite unique to Christianity and is vitally related to the indwelling Trinity within us. It confesses that we human beings have been meant by God to live in harmony with the entire material world. It professes the belief that God's redeeming love extends, not merely to the spiritual side of mankind, but also embraces the materiality of the whole cosmos. We in God's creative Word are all interconnected: angels, human beings, and all the subhuman cosmos.

We cannot be redeemed unless the world that made us what we are is also brought into the same redemption. The good news is that Jesus Christ is already here bringing about the kingdom of God in our lives and, through us, bringing it about in the entire world. We can be sidetracked from the essential elements of this important teaching of the second coming of Christ if we take too literally the scriptural images of life after death, as though they will happen exclusively at the end of our human history.

By focusing upon the *Parousia* as an eschatological fulfillment that is dependent upon our daily living in the death-resurrection of Jesus Lord, we will be living this doctrine now and, in the best way, we will prepare for his ultimate coming in glory.

The End of the World

The end of the world is not tied to some mathematical equation concerning the heat-death of the planet that science can predict for us. It is tied intrinsically to our history as persons who make decisions to live in love or in fear and selfishness. The end of the world is tied, not merely to God's ultimate decree, but to our human ability to form free decisions as to the direction of this universe. Thus we can never know when the fullness of this world will come and when the transformation of this material existence will move the cosmos into a new spiritual existence.

Jesus, in the apocalyptic discourses found in the three synoptic Gospels of Mark, Matthew, and Luke, had much to say about the end of the world. He, or the authors of these Gospels, used the eschatological imagery already found in the prophets Isaiah, Ezekiel, and Daniel, along with the apocryphal writings, such as the Books of Enoch, that were so popular from the second century BC through the first century AD among the Jews of Palestine. Jesus himself clearly states: "But about that day or hour no one knows, neither the angels in heaven, nor the Son, but only the Father" (Mark 13:32).

The Entire Cosmos Is Linked to Christ

The important scriptural message about the end of the world that Jesus leaves with us through the teaching of the Evangelists is that the end of the world is firmly and indissolubly linked to the person of Jesus Christ, who, as the Messiah, the Lord of the universe, will take the kingdom of God up with him to share in his power and his glory. He has sovereignty over the entire world, and this reign will be manifested at the end of the world, so that all nations can see that Jesus Christ is the Lord, the one to whom power and dominion have been given by the Father to unite all things into a loving submission to God (1 Cor 15:28).

The other message about the end of the world, as we have already indicated several times, is the urgency of vigilance in the now moment because the Son is already coming into his fullness through his loving members, who cooperate with him to build his Body. He is hidden, but is already bringing about the glorification of the universe. "Watch, be vigilant" is the message about the end of the world. But it is also a message of joyful hope. *Maranatha!*—"Come, Lord Jesus" (1 Cor 16:22)—is the hopeful expectancy that gives us courage in the dark night to await with joy the coming of the dawn of the full light of Christ as Love.

With great longing in our hearts we, too, are to go forth into our world and to unveil the hidden presence of the risen Lord as we seek lovingly to serve each other and, therefore, to bring Christ to full maturity.

Final Judgment

The future final judgment of the world, passed by the Son of God, Jesus Christ, has also been an important belief in the Christian message about the end of the world. Jesus is seen in the eschatological discourse in Matthew's Gospel as gathering the entire world, "all the nations," into a final judgment and sifting those who will be "saved" from those who will be condemned:

> When the Son of Man comes in his glory...before him will be gathered all the nations, and he will separate them one from another, as a shepherd separates the sheep from the goats....Then the King will say to those at his right hand: "Come, O blessed of my Father, inherit the kingdom prepared for you from the foundation of the world." (Matt 25:31–34)

This is more than a static moment at the end of the world and more than a judgment on the particulars of our good and bad deeds done while on earth. It is in and through this judgment that God will establish the heavenly community, the ultimate state of his kingdom of heaven. When God manifests himself in the fullness of Christ, then every one of us will be exposed and seen in the light of Christ. Our identity will be seen in the degree to which we allow the love of Christ's Spirit to create our true selves in him through our loving relationships with the other members of Christ's Body.

The consummation of the world will be a judgment. Those human beings who have lived their baptism through death to selfishness and in loving service to others will enter into a life of intimate union with the Trinity, with all other angelic and human spirits, and with the entire universe, that we could call the state of heaven. They will know that that state was theirs while they lived on this earth in love toward others. Those others who have encased themselves in self-centered love will be judged to have only that. They will find that their early lives prepared them by their free choices to a limited view of reality. This is what we could call the state of Hell.

Christ, in a special manner, will be manifested as the Universal Judge. "He is the one ordained by God to be judge of the living and the dead" (Acts 10:42). This will be his crowning victory over sin and death and will be seen in the intimate union between the members of his Body, the angels, and the saints, and their Head, Christ. Here, in the final judgment, we see the fullness of his Lordship exercised over the entire universe. We see the full meaning of his resurrection, and it carries with it a sharing of glory and power to all who have shared in his sufferings, death, and resurrection to love others. Paul writes:

> What then are we to say? Should we continue in sin in order that grace may abound? By no means! How can we who died to sin go on living in it? Do you not know that all of us who have been baptized into Christ Jesus were baptized into his death? Therefore we have been buried with him by baptism into death, so that, just as Christ was raised from the dead by the glory of the Father, so we too might walk in newness of life. (Rom 6:1–4)

Final Glory

If we are guided by the experience of the resurrection of Jesus Christ, who with the Father and the Holy Spirit, abides in our present now of our earthly existence, we will see that we are already "becoming" a part of the total, glorified Christ. This final glory of the Body of Christ risen is being realized even now, as we learn to surrender ourselves in loving service to each other through the Spirit of the risen Lord. The resurrection is a process of the coming into glory of the full Christ.

This comes about gradually through the symbol of the cross and death, a symbol of continued purification and conversion away from dark egoism to embrace and live in the inner light of Jesus risen and living within us. Resurrection is a series of "yeses" to the dictates of Jesus' Spirit.

Heaven Is the Union of the Body of Christ

As we let go of our pseudocontrol over our existence and independence from God, neighbor, and our material world, and "pass over" to a greater union in a loving I-Thou relationship in a larger We-Community, the Body of Christ, we are entering into the state we call heaven, that is, the state of oneness with Christ and the Heavenly Father by the binding love of the Holy Spirit and all the members who make up the Body of Christ.

This means that we become "reconcilers" with Christ of the entire world. God gave us this work of handing on this reconciliation, in this present earthly existence and in our heavenly existence in the life to come (2 Cor 5:18). Both in this present existence and in the life to come before the fullness of Christ's glory is manifested, we have the dignity, by our service within the Body of Christ, to extend the reconciliation by Christ of all things back to the Father.

The life of glory is both a sharing in the corporate fullness of the Body of Christ and a finding of one's unique, personal fullness as a living member of that Body of Christ, with special gifts developed through loving service toward others.

Love Ever Grows

St. Paul assures us that, in the life to come, all other things will pass away except love. "Love does not come to an end" (1 Cor 13:8). Resurrection and our entrance into the kingdom of God are always happening, even now, as we live in the Spirit's love. Heaven is where God is being recognized as present and active in his uncreated love energies. He calls us to respond to his love and to accept a share in the risen Body of Christ as we humbly seek to serve each other in building the Body of Christ.

We can see that both in our life now with the indwelling Trinity and in the heavenly life, there must never be any attempt to be exclusively in a vertical relation with God-Trinity that cuts us off from loving service of human beings and all other creatures of God. Paul assures us that healthy members come in love to aid the needy. Love grows in loving service. Resurrection is love in action to do the will of God. We are sharing in Christ's resurrection, as we not only die to any selfishness, but also as we live to glorify the Blessed Trinity. This means that we live in loving service to bring the Body of Christ to its full resurrection and glory.

Heaven Is Not an Old Folks' Home

The kingdom of heaven is the entrance into the resurrection of Christ as we discover God in his unique love for each person whom we encounter. This interaction begins in this earthly existence and continues in the life to come. As we positively allow the power of God in Christ Jesus through his ever-present gift of his Holy Spirit to interact in all of us, our power to love increases. We experience the resurrection of the Lord exerting his power of glory upon us. As we grow in love, the resurrectional power of Jesus becomes more powerful and transformative in our lives. The Body of Christ also grows more full of glory and power.

God is becoming God and Jesus is becoming the resurrection, as we become living signs of the new creation by the love we allow to shine forth from our lives into the lives of others. We are daily destroying the temple with all its built-in idols, as we allow Jesus risen to bring about the fulfillment of his words: "Destroy this sanctuary, and in three days I will raise it up" (John 2:19).

Living in the Mystery of Love

To let go and live in the mystery of love is to touch the wounds of the risen Lord and know that God is raising his Son to new power and glory by bringing greater oneness in love among the members in oneness with their Head, Jesus Christ. The miracle of the resurrection is happening at every moment of our daily life and also in the existence we call "heaven," as we are open to God's Word speaking in his creative acts of raising us up to new levels of sharing in his resurrectional, transforming love.

This moment is always a new beginning, the first day of eternity. Heaven is growing and all this happens, as we members live death-resurrection in this present "now" moment. "As long as we love one another, God will live in us and his love will be complete in us" (1 John 4:12). We can interpret these beautiful words to mean "as long as we love one another, Christ is more completely being risen in power and glory."

We will always be part of a New Jerusalem that is being fashioned whenever members in Christ love one another. In joy and peace we can say "No" to Babylon and "Yes" to the New Jerusalem, God's new creation. Rooted in the human situation of God's creation, we live in love and through service, we seek for that New City that awaits us and, yet, mysteriously is already here among us (Rev 21:3–7).

Eye Has Not Seen

What strange ideas most of us Christians have about heaven. We usually lock ourselves into earthly experiences of space and time and merely project the same ideas onto an experience that has no space and time, and is unlimited. Our sugary, self-centered ideas of heaven do not match up with God's revealed Word in scripture. The essence of heaven is among "the things that no eye has seen and no ear has heard, things beyond the mind of man, all that God has prepared for those who love him" (1 Cor 2:9). "Yes, the heavens are as high above earth as my ways are above your ways, my thoughts above your thoughts" (Isa 55:9).

I Believe in Hell and Purgatory

It is important that we ponder heaven with clear and correct ideas for we will then be guided as to how we can now best live on earth. Heaven is no material place to which we "go" after we are purified for a certain number of days or years. We will not pop out of "purgatory" and zoom over to heaven.

Do not misunderstand me. Yes, I truly believe that hell really exists, but hell is a solipsistic world that we, while living on this earth, have created by focusing upon our own independence and false pride and turning away from God's salvific plan to continually become made by sanctifying graces "according to God's image and likeness that is Jesus Christ" (Col 1:15). I definitely believe in purgatory as a merciful period of "therapy" to find Christ in all the earthly thoughts, words, and deeds that we experienced on earth without discovering Christ as the Word who is the Communicator of the Father. All of our earthly experiences are stored up in our consciousness and unconscious, and influenced forming who we are when we leave this earthly existence.[1]

When we strip away all our earthly imaginings about heaven as an objective, material place where we will be eternally happy without anymore suffering, and begin to live God's revelations through Christ, we will discover heaven primarily to consist of all the loving relationships we have experienced on earth and to continue to grow in loving service to build the Body of Christ. The idea of heaven we entertain and live by should see God as the goal of all our earthly strivings. The Blessed Trinity is the complete reason for God's creating us. God is not only the beginning and end of all reality, but he is our loving Father through Jesus Christ in their Spirit.

God Has Created Us to Share the Holy Trinity

We will realize that we were created out of God's trinitarian community of Father, Son, and Holy Spirit to share intimately in that very life of God. We will be driven by an inner force, a burning, passionate desire to know and lovingly serve God in the deepest intimacy. He who is love (1 John 4:8) wants us to enter into that ongoing life of love of the Trinity.

We Shall Be in Christ

What we have stressed already in all the preceding chapters from scripture and the teachings of the Church, we will in heaven realize and live out in the power and glory of the indwelling Trinity: the fulfillment of our life in Christ, which baptism brought about, as we were incorporated into his Body, the Church. Heaven is the kingdom of God within us, whereby, incorporated into Christ, we are made really one with him through his Spirit by an inner regeneration (John 3:3, 5). Thus we are able to live in the trinitarian community.

The central message of the preaching of Christ is about heaven and his making it possible through his Spirit that we might find God's community of the Trinity living within and around us. We become empowered by that Trinity to bring forth other living communities of one and many in the power of God's Spirit of Love. God, as community, is already infinitely loving each one of us from within, through God's sanctifying graces.

As we open up to his love and care for us, in and through Christ and his Spirit, we are commissioned, both in this earthly existence and in our continued life after death, to build the community of the Body of Christ. We live for others by laboring to build a social order grounded on justice and love, humility and meekness, respect for the oneness of all creatures in Christ and for their uniqueness in his creation. As members of his Body, we will seek always to serve each other's uniqueness in love.

Interpersonal Relationships Always Growing

Most theologians before Vatican II, in teaching about the essence of our eternal happiness in heaven, described this in static terms of our "seeing" God's essence in the beatific vision. God's perfection was perfect and immutable, and such static fixity was deemed the ultimate. Christians today yawn before such seriousness, as theologians in the past battled among themselves to explain just how it was possible for us to see God, "face to face," in the beatific vision.

Our modern world explodes into such fresh and exciting richness that to consider heaven in any static and immobile terms has very little meaning today. Heaven as a place to which the "saved" go to gaze upon the essence of God through the beatific vision is being replaced by a more dynamic concept of a state of continued growth as God, angels, and human beings lovingly interact to bring forth God's initial creation into ever-increasing beauty and harmony and unity in love.

A Continued Growth in Love of God and Neighbor

Far from being the static "vision" of gazing upon three immobile Persons of the Trinity, the beatific vision can become for us a dynamic and exciting process of continued growth in love of God and of neighbor. Caught up within the very dialectic of the Godhead, who is eternally moving from Silence to Speech, from perfect repose and motionlessness to sharing love in movement toward another, we, too, live in the blissful tension of peaceful repose and movement toward others in love.

How exciting to think that heaven will be a state of continuous growth in loving "towardness" toward God and all his creatures, especially in loving service toward other human beings and not, after all, to be an "old folks' home"! St. Gregory of Nyssa describes true perfection in heaven as "never to stop growing toward what is better and never to place any limit on perfection."[2]

Grace, or the life of God within human beings and angels, both in this earthly life and in heaven, presupposes growth in accepting a loving relationship with God. And this means, above all, to accept the necessity of constantly moving in love toward God and neighbor.

If God is love and is limitless in his goodness and beauty and love toward us, our desire must also be limitless. The very unrest, the stretching forth to higher perfection, to greater union with the Trinity, is more than moving from one stage of perfection to another. It is more than a mere, static vision of God's beauty. God is eternally at rest, yet he exists always in an outgoing motion of love to share himself with others.

Continued Growth in Freedom

After you and I as individual persons have been purified in this life and in the life to come through the therapy of purgatory, we will stretch out ever more toward God, who continually calls each person to forget "what lies behind and strain...forward to what lies ahead" (Phil 3:13), as Paul tells us.

Gregory Nyssa, inspired by Paul's mystical process that knows no end of growth, writes in a similar vein: "And, thus, the soul moves ceaselessly upwards, always reviving its tension for its onward flight by means of the progress it has already realized. Indeed, it is only spiritual activity that nourishes its force by exercise; it does not slacken its tension by action, but rather increases it."[3]

Such spiritual growth, stretching in love toward greater union with the triune God and with other angels, saints, and the whole human race, is what it means to be human. You become human, not only in the desiring, but also by God's condescending to give of himself always in newer and more amazing ways to you, who seek after him with all your heart. "Blessed are those who hunger and thirst for righteousness, for they will be filled" (Matt 5:6).

This is the opinion of theologian Piet Schoonenberg, SJ, who insists on a growth process in the life to come in heaven: "A certain growth also remains possible in the final fulfillment. Otherwise, we would perhaps cease to be human. Just as life constantly rediscovers itself from the past into the future, so we shall constantly rediscover our past and present in and from God in new and surprising ways."[4]

Love Will Grow As We Seek to Serve Others

Can you, therefore, imagine that your purified, unselfish love for God will not enter into an ever-increasing, evolutionary growth in knowledge of God or loving surrender of self to serve God and neighbor through loving service? Redemption should, perhaps, be better conceived of, not as a fixed state of beatific repose, but as a growing process of discovering the love of God, both as manifested by his direct revelation of himself to us in his trinitarian relationships and as manifested in his participated beauty in creation, especially in his angels and saintly human beings.

Loving Service to Others

With the divine energies of God's love always surrounding you, both in this earthly existence and in the transformed world of heaven always calling you to respond to his Word, you reach the highest development by your continued cooperation to work with God's energetic presence in self-emptying love for others. As you cooperate with God's graces, you will come to meet God and glorify him by your loving service toward other persons, both angels and human beings.

True prayer and sanctity, both in this earthly life and in heaven, must be measured exclusively by the degree of charity and humility possessed by the individual and shown in loving actions toward others. The love of God experienced in prayerful adoration before God "urges" you, to quote St. Paul's term, to go out from yourself in humble service to all who need more of God's love, who need more sharing of God's beauty and perfection through your extension of his active love for others.

Heaven can be no exception to the standard given us by Christ for life on earth, of measuring love for God by our love and service shown to our neighbor. You know whether the Trinity abides in you by the love that you have for one another. True prayer is always begetting, becoming the other in greater unity of love that alone can be realized by humble service toward the other.

Spiritualization of God's Creation

Let us seek to imagine at least what communion among the saints and angels in heaven with the Holy Trinity will be like. Let us keep in mind the need we have to move always beyond the limitations of our earthly experiences when we think of heaven. Karl Rahner gives us this important caution: "It is a priori senseless to ask where Heaven is, if by this 'where' we are to understand a location in our physical, spatial world."[5]

We cannot imagine what a spiritual body or a spiritualized person in glory will mean in being toward others who also are spiritualized. As we have already cautioned against "materializing" the indwelling Trinity in our material bodies, so also we must avoid imagining life in heaven using only our experiences from our earthly communion with God and other human beings.

Gone will be the aggressive attacks on others, now replaced by a Christ-like gentleness as you open up to receive God's diaphanous presence, shining toward you, through the prism of each human and angelic spirit encountered. The Christ in you embraces the Christ in your neighbor, and you respond with the excitement of new discoveries of God's beauty in your oneness in Christ.

No Strangers in Heaven

No longer is the other a stranger, a simple object "over there," separated from you. Others become your brothers and sisters as you and they are seen as vital members of Christ. You discover your uniqueness as you live in the dynamic of Christ's Spirit of "passing-over" from yourself to lovingly serve others and, thus, you build up the total Christ by every thought, word, and action.

No longer will there be two commandments: to love God and then to love your neighbor. If you truly are loving God and experiencing his love for you, you will be loving God in all persons and experiencing his love as you accept their love. Each love relationship will be unique and God-revealing. Such love experienced will call out a new impulse to give yourself lovingly in service to others.

Through purification, Christ will have entered into all of your earthly experiences once your self-centeredness has yielded to Christ-centeredness. You will, therefore, be able to share your past experiences with others. All will be unto God's glory. Nothing will be merely "natural" or "secular." God will be "all in all" as you can share your experiences in education, travel, in human loves, in sufferings, and in discovering God's beauty in all human experiences, no matter how insignificant they may have appeared to you while you lived on earth.

Developing Our Talents and Sharing Them

All persons in Christ will develop even further talents and abilities in loving service to others. What would prevent Mozart and Beethoven from producing even more God-revealing music than they did on earth? The beautiful and famous saints, like the apostles and the martyrs, and the unknown "little" saints, who served Christ and his Body in hidden fidelity and great love, will all vie with each other to be the humblest and most zealous to love and serve others. Everyone will be content with his or her charisms. In heaven, there will be no jealousy or competition, but only humble, loving service.

How angels and human beings will intercommunicate in heaven has not been revealed to us by God. That is part of what awaits us. But we can truly believe that "communion of saints" means greater oneness in Christ's Body in intimate union with him as our Head.

Heaven: A New Beginning of True Life

Heaven is not the end of our existence, our finally coming home to rest eternally. It is the beginning of true life, God's life, which has already begun on this earth. It is like an onion made up of layer after layer and consists of nothing but circles of layers. To go deeper and deeper into God-Trinity's love is to make each circle larger than the last.

It is a dance that starts even in this life, as we begin to love and dance in joyful harmony with other persons in true godly love. An ever-widening circle of love extends outward to embrace other dancers. The dance goes on forever; new dancers join us as the circle of our love, which is one with the love of Christ in us, the Holy Spirit, extends itself to embrace the whole world of God's dancing creatures.

Our primary focus of activity is to give glory to God-Trinity and to enjoy God and all his creatures in him. This can have very little appeal to persons who on earth have never thirsted for God and have not drunk from the living waters of God's love. Rooted in God's being as the Source of our identity, we will explore the many ways God concretely loves us. We will discover, as we have also discovered in some limited way in this earthly life, his outpouring love, first, into our own life and in so many different ways.

We will be amazed as we discover the converging of all those love moments to allow us to enjoy God in this now-eternal moment of love. As we know and love ourselves in God's tremendous and unique love for each of us, we will still see our love for ourselves, God, and others needing development. In communion with the angels and saints, will we know and want to know facts about their lives, their experiences? Yes, but only in the measure that we wish lovingly to serve them through such knowledge and praise God for his active love in those experiences. There will be no place for idle curiosity stemming from pride and selfishness. We will relax and be honest without any need to protect our "interests" at the cost of true union in love with others. We will live according to Paul's injunction: "But speaking the truth in love, we must grow up in every way into him who is the head, into Christ, from whom the whole body...promotes the body's growth in building itself up in love" (Eph 4:15–17).

We will see the secret happiness that we glimpsed on earth from time to time and we will learn that the more we live to serve another in love, the more we receive God in that person. We give in service, not for any self-centered advantages, but only to draw out happiness in others. Heaven is truly a door (Rev 4:1) that opens before us so that we can humbly and joyfully enter into God's reality. And part of God's real world, as Jesus has revealed to us, is that God has created all things in and through his Son (John 1:3).

Yet we are called to be "co-creators" with Christ to evolve the created, material world in all its diversity and complexity into a oneness in Christ unto God's eternal praise and glory.

The Cosmic Christ

Christian doctrine holds a basic optimism toward God's material creation that he sees always as "good" (Gen 1:18). It teaches in apocalyptic imagery that Christ will come at the end of time to transform this material universe by bringing it to its completion in and through himself. Just how this will be accomplished has not been revealed in detail. Paul writes: "in Christ God was reconciling the world to himself" (2 Cor 5:19). Each individual member of Christ has a role to play on this earth and in the glorious life to come in the reconciliation of the cosmos to Christ's power and rule. The Body of Christ will be filled up, not only with living human members submitted to Christ's reconciling power, but through their cooperation in relationship to the material world, they will lead in a mysterious way the created world back to the Father in Christ through the overshadowing of the Sanctifier of the universe, the Holy Spirit. "And he has put all things under his feet and has made him the head over all things for the church, which is his body, the fullness of him who fills all in all" (Eph 1:22–23).

A Transfigured Creation

No longer will there be chaos, dissension, and aversion of the created, subhuman world from God. The whole brute world will have reached its completion in being transfigured from its deformity, its "vanity," as Paul calls it, into a "renovated creation." Our world will never be annihilated, but rather it will be transfigured. There will be a communion of saints with the spiritualized world, as the saints will cooperate to evolve that world into a manifestation of Christ's power and dominion even over the subhuman cosmos.

We are in need of recapturing the vision of St. Paul, St. John, and the early Christian Fathers of the Church, especially the early Greek Fathers. They saw in Jesus Christ the "Alpha," the beginning, in whom all things were created (John 1:2). They also saw him as the "Omega," the goal, the end toward which every finite creature was moving.

We Christians will work actively to move the created world from death and corruption, the wages of sin, to incorruptible life in Christ.

Jesus Christ, vibrantly alive and inserted into the material world and actively with our cooperation, is the key to true progress and the full meaning of this created cosmos. The whole creation, including human beings, who freely submit to the guidance of Jesus Christ, is now accomplishing this in the created universe. But its completion and fulfillment will be a part of heaven and our human cooperation to complete God-Trinity's initial plan to create all things in God's Word (John 1:2).

Conclusion

I would like to end this last chapter on the subject of heaven and the life to come as the fulfillment of what we have seen in all the preceding chapters of this book on the mystery of the indwelling Holy Trinity in us by quoting from St. Paul:

> So if anyone is in Christ, there is a new creation: everything old has passed away; see, everything has become new! All this is from God, who reconciled us to himself through Christ, and has given us the ministry of reconciliation; that is, in Christ God was reconciling the world to himself, not counting their trespasses against them, and entrusting the message of reconciliation to us. So we are ambassadors for Christ, since God is making his appeal through us; we entreat you on behalf of Christ, be reconciled to God. For our sake he made him to be sin who knew no sin, so that in him we might become the righteousness of God. (2 Cor 5:17–21)

Notes

Epigraph

1. St. Symeon the New Theologian, *Hymns of Divine Love*, trans. George A. Maloney, SJ (Denville, NJ: Dimension Books, 1975), Hymn 52, p. 52.

Chapter One

1. For a penetrating, Jungian development of this myth, see Robert A. Johnson, *He: Understanding Masculine Psychology* (New York: Perennial Library, 1974).
2. St. Augustine, *Confessiones* 10.27.38, Patrologia Latina, hereafter PL (Paris, 1844–64), 32:795.
3. Emil Brunner, *Man in Revolt* (London: The Lutterworth Press, 1953), 97.
4. M. C. Richards, *The Crossing Point* (Middletown, CT: Wesleyan University Press, 1980), 60.
5. Gerald Manley Hopkins, "The Hurranhing," in *Poems by Gerald Manley Hopkins,* ed. Norman H. MacKenzie (London: The Folio Society, 1974) Poem 23, p.70
6. Evelyn Underhill, *The School of Charity and the Mystery of Sacrifice* (New York: Longmans, Green & Co., 1956), 235.
7. *Augustine of Hippo: Selected Writings*, trans. Mary Clark (New York/Ramsey, NJ: Paulist Press, 1984), 81.
8. Walter Hilton, *The Scale of Perfection,* ed. Gerard Sitwell (London: Thurgarton, 1953), 35.
9. Dag Hammarskjold, *Markings* (London: Faber & Faber, 1964), 58.

NOTES

Chapter Two

1. Søren Kierkegaard, *The Sickness unto Death* (Garden City, NY: Doubleday, 1954), 10.

2. Gregory Nazianzus, Homilia XLII, 15, in Patrologia Graeca, hereafter PG (Paris, 1856–66), 36:476.

3. Friedrich Nietzsche, source of quote unknown.

4. For a more detailed presentation of the personal divine relationships within the Trinity, see my two books *Invaded by God* (Denville, NJ: Dimension Books, 1979) and *God's Community of Love* (Hyde Park, NY: New City Press, 1995).

5. Gabriel Marcel, *Metaphysical Journal,* trans. Bernard Wall (Chicago: H. Regnery Co., 1952), 26, 147, 221.

6. Hilary of Poitiers, *The Trinity* 2.6.41, The Fathers of the Church, no. 25 (Washington, DC: Catholic University Press, 1954).

7. Otto Michel, "Oikonomia," in *Theological Dictionary of the New Testament,* hereafter *TDNT,* vol. 5, ed. Gerhard Friedrich (Grand Rapids, MI: Eerdmans Co., 1995), 157–59.

8. Vladimir Lossky, *The Mystical Theology of the Eastern Church* (Naperville, IL: Clarke Ltd., 1957), 71.

9. Karl Rahner, *The Trinity* (New York: Herder & Herder, 1969), 22.

10. Ibid., 101.

11. See George A. Maloney, *A Theology of Uncreated Energies* (Milwaukee, WI: Marquette University Press, 1978).

12. St. Irenaeus, *Adversus Haereses* V, 28, 4, in *The Ante-Nicene Fathers,* hereafter *ANF,* vol. 1, eds. A. Roberts and J. Donaldson (Grand Rapids, MI: Eerdmans, 1958), 557.

Chapter Three

1. Rahner, *The Trinity,* 10–11.

2. Luis M. Bermejo, *The Spirit of Life* (India: Gujarat Sahitya Prakash, 1987), 10.

3. Richard of St. Victor, *De Trinitate* III, 19; PL, p. 196, 915B–930D.

4. St. Ignatius of Antioch, *Letter to the Magnesians* VIII, 2; PG 5:765.

5. Richard of St. Victor, *De Trinitate*, p. 138.

6. Ibid., 147.

Chapter Four

1. Heribert Mühlen, SJ, *Der Heilige Geist als Person* (Münster: Aschendorff, 1966).

2. Dietrich von Hildebrand, *Metaphysik der Gemeinschaft* (Regensberg: J. Habbel, 1955).

3. Wilhelm von Humboldt, *Gesammelte Schriften*, 17 vols., 1903–36 (Berlin: Akademie d. Wisenschaften, 1968).

4. Ibid., "Uber die Verwandtschaft der Ortsadverbien mit dem Pronomen in cinigen Sprachen," in *Gesammellte Schriften*, 304 ff, vol. unknown.

5. Hildebrand, *Metaphysik*, 34.

6. George A. Maloney, *The Cosmic Christ: From Paul to Teilhard de Chardin* (New York: Sheed & Ward, 1968), 196.

7. Jaroslav Pelikan, *The Spirit of Eastern Christendom*, The Christian Tradition: A History of the Development of Doctrine, vol. 2, (Chicago: The University of Chicago Press, 1974), 183–98.

8. George A. Maloney, *The Spirit Broods Over the World* (Staten Island, NY: Alba House, 1993), especially Chaps. 1 and 3.

Chapter Five

1. This Sanskrit text of five thousand years ago was kindly translated by a fellow Jesuit educated in India.

2. St. Maximus the Confessor, *Quaestiones ad. Thalassium* 21; PG 90:312–16.

3. *Epistola* XXI; PG 91:312–16.

4. St. Athanasius, *De Incarnatione Verbi*, PG 25:192B.

5. St. Cyril of Alexandria, *De recta Fide ad Theodosium*, PG 76:1177A.

6. Jules Gross, *Divinisation du Chrétien d'aprés les Peres grecs* (Paris: J. Gabalda, 1938).

7. *St. Maximus the Confessor: The Ascetic Life and the Four Centuries on Charity*, trans. and annot. Polycarp Sherwood, OSB (Paris: Garbalda, 1938), 231n292.

8. Paul Evdokimov, "L'Esprit Saint et L'Eglise d'apres la tradition liturgique," in *L'Esprit Saint et L'Eglise*. Actes du Symposium organise par l'Academie Internationale des Sciences Religieuses (Paris, 1969).

Chapter Six

1. Basil, "Epistle to Amphilochius," cited by G. Habra, "The Patristic Sources of the Doctrine of Gregory Palamas on the Divine Energies," in *Eastern Churches Quarterly* 12 (1957–58).

2. Basil, *Epistola* 234; PG 32:869.

3. "Mystical Theology," PG 3, Part 1; and "Divine Names," PG 3, Part 1.

4. "Divine Names," PG 3, Part 1.

5. Ibid.

6. John Meyendorff, *A Study of Gregory Palamas* (London: Faith Press, 1964), 221–22.

7. Archbishop Joseph Raya, *The Face of God* (Denville, NJ: Dimension Books 1976), 37–38.

8. Meyendorff, *Study*, 218n63.

9. Basil Krivoshein, "The Ascetical and Theological Teaching of Gregory Palamas," in *The Eastern Churches Quarterly* 3 (1938–39): 15.

10. Gregoire Palamas, *Les Triads pour la defense des saints Hesychastes*, 3 vols, ed. J. Meyendorff (Louvain, France: Spicilegium Sacrum Lovaniense, 1959), *Triad* II, 3, 67.

11. M. F. Hussey, "The Persons-Energy Structure in the Theology of St. Gregory Palamas," in *St. Vladimir's Theological Quarterly* 18 (1974): 3.

12. Palamas, *Against Akindynos* II, 9, in *Works*, ed. P. K. Christos (Greece: University of Thessalonika Press, 1966).

13. Ibid., III, 8.

14. *Triads* II, 3, 77.

15. V. Lossky, *Mystical Theology*, 162–63.

16. St. Thomas Aquinas, *Summa Theologiae* 1a 2ae, Q. 109, intro., 2 ans.; Q. 110, 1 ans.

17. Rahner, *Trinity*, 23.

18. Karl Rahner, *Nature & Grace* (London: Sheed & Ward, 1963), 24.

19. Ibid.

20. St. Symeon, Catecheses 24, cited by G. Maloney, *Mystic of Fire and Light* (Denville, NJ: Dimension Books, 1975), 72.

21. Krivoshein, "Ascetical and Theological," 28.

22. P. Camelot, OP, "*La theologie de l'Image de Dieu,*" in *Revue des Sciences Phil. Et Theol.* (1956): 470–71.

Chapter Seven

1. George A. Maloney, *Entering into the Heart of Jesus* (Staten Island, NY: Alba House, 1981), 107–8.

2. Raymond E. Brown, ed., *The Gospel according to John XIII–XXI* (New York: Doubleday, 1970), 668–84.

Chapter Eight

1. Carolyn Osiek, RSCJ, *Galatians*, in New Testament Message, Vol. 12 (Wilmington, DE: Michael Glazier, 1980), 1–4.

Chapter Nine

1. The word *Docetism* is derived from the Greek word

dokesis, meaning "appearance," and refers to those who denied the reality of Christ's physical incarnation. *Monophysitism* is derived from the Greek words *monos*, meaning "one," and *physis*, meaning "nature." It refers to the fifth-century heresy that maintained that there was but a single nature in Christ, that is, his humanity was subsumed into his divinity, or that the two natures in Christ made up only one composite nature. It was condemned in the Council of Chalcedon (451 AD).

2. Arianism was a heresy condemned in the first two ecumenical councils of Nicaea (325 AD) and Constantinople (AD 381).

3. Three Catholic theologians who hold a similar view are Hans Küng, Piet Schoonenberg, and Jon Sobrino.

4. Louis Bouyer, *Eucharist* (Notre Dame, IN: University of Notre Dame Press, 1968), 467.

5. Didache 9, trans. Henry Bettinson, W. J. Sparrow-Simpson and W. K. Lowther Clarke, eds., in *Documents of the Christian World* (London: Society for Promoting Christian Knowledge, 1959), 90.

6. P. Bernadot, OP, *From Holy Communion to the Trinity* (Westminster, MD: The Newman Press, 1948).

Chapter Ten

1. There seems to be very few books recently published on this important gift of joy. See G. A. Maloney, SJ, *That Your Joy May Be Complete* (Hyde Park, NY: New City Press, 1997) for a select bibliography on this topic.

2. On the subject of absolute surrender, see A. Murray, *Absolute Surrender* (Chicago: Moody Press, no date).

3. For scholarly research on the subject of "joy" as found among the New Testament writers, see articles on *Chara (Xara)* and derivatives by Hans Conzelmann and Walther Zimmerli, in *TDNT,* vol. IX, pp. 366–71 and 391–406.

Chapter Eleven

1. Cited by Maria F. Mahoney, *The Meaning in Dreams & Dreaming* (Secaucus, NJ: The Citadel Press, 1976), 138.
2. These ideas are more fully developed in *Woman Is the Glory of Man,* E. Danniel & B. Olivier (Westminster, MD: Newman Press, 1966).
3. Quoted by Geoffrey Grigson, *G. M. Hopkins* (London: Longmans, Green & Co., 1955), 22.
4. Cited by Raoul Plus, SJ, *God Within Us* (London: Burns, Oates & Washbourne Co., 1929), 4.
5. St. Ignatius of Antioch, ANF, 53.
6. M. V. Bernadot, OP, *Holy Communion,* p. 47.
7. Ibid.
8. Blessed Elizabeth of the Trinity, ODC, *The Doctrine of the Divine Indwelling* (Westminster, MD: Newman Press, 1950), 57.
9. Two typical theologians who presented in their works a summary collection of the numerous Scholastic theologians of the middle of the twentieth century are Robt. Gleason, SJ, in *The Dwelling Spirit* (Staten Island, NY: Alba House, 1960) and Francis L. B. Cunningham, OP, in *The Indwelling Trinity* (Dubuque, IA: Priory Press, 1955).
10. Cited by Plus, *God Within Us,* 125.
11. Cited by Bernadot, *From Holy Communion,* 43.
12. Elizabeth of the Trinity, *Divine Indwelling,* 36 .
13. St. John of the Cross, *The Living Flame of Love,* in *Collected Works of St. John of the Cross* (Washington, DC: ICS Publications, 1973), 604–5.
14. Ibid., 607.
15. Brother Lawrence, *The Practice of the Presence of God* (New York/Ramsey, NJ: Paulist Press, 1978), 127.
16. Dr. Frank C. Laubach, *Open Windows, Swinging Doors* (Glendale, CA: C/L Publications, 1955), 27 ff.

NOTES

17. Paul Tillich, *The Protestant Era* (Chicago: Chicago University Press, 1959), 57. Cf. G. A. Maloney, SJ, *Called to Be Free* (Staten Island, NY: Alba House, 2001), 67–73.

18. B. Bartmann, cited in Alfred Wikenhauser, *Pauline Mysticism: Christ in the Mystical Teaching of St. Paul* (New York: Herder & Herder, 1956), 93–94.

19. Leszek Kolakowski, "Quietism," in *The Encyclopedia of Religion*, vol. 12 (New York: Macmillan Publishing Co., 1987), 153–55.

20. P. De Jaegher, SJ, source unknown.

21. In the Old and New Testaments in Hebrew the word *heart (qerev)* is the place where God actively implants his moral laws and empowers the individual to act righteously in keeping with his laws. It is the heart that is the center of one's religious relationships with God and neighbor. In the heart one learns to fear God and be obedient by acting faithfully according to the Hesed Covenant God has freely entered into with his chosen people. See G. Maloney, *Deep Calls to Deep* (Denville, NJ: Dimension Books, 1993), especially Ch. 4, "What Does Heart Mean?"

Chapter Twelve

1. George A. Maloney, SJ, *The Everlasting Now* (Notre Dame, IN: Ave Maria Press, 1980), and *Death, Where Is Your Sting* (Staten Island, NY: Alba House, 1984).

2. St. Gregory of Nyssa, *On Perfection*, trans. V. W. Callahan, Fathers of the Church, vol. 58 (Washington, DC: Catholic University of America Press, 1967), 122.

3. St. Gregory Nyssa, *Life of Moses*, in *From Glory to Glory*, trans. and ed. J. Danielou and H. Musurillo (New York: Charles Scribner's Sons, 1961), 144.

4. Piet Schoonenberg, SJ, "I Believe in Eternal Life," in *Dogma: The Problem of Eschatology*, Concilium 1 (New York: Paulist Press, 1969), 110.

5. Karl Rahner, SJ, *Theological Investigations*, vol. 11 (Baltimore: Helicon Press, 1964), 215.